THIRTY MILLION STRONG

Reclaiming the Hispanic Image in American Culture

NICOLÁS KANELLOS

FULCRUM PUBLISHING
GOLDEN, COLORADO

Book design by Alyssa Pumphrey

Cover image © 1998 Denver Civic Theatre. *Mural designed and super-vised by Andy Mendoza. Art contributed by children and members of the community. Located on the south wall of the Denver Civic Theatre, 721 Santa Fe Drive, Denver, Colorado.*

Library of Congress Cataloging-in-Publication Data

Kanellos, Nicolás.
   Thirty million strong : reclaiming the Hispanic image in American culture / Nicolás Kanellos.
      p.   cm.
   Includes bibliographical references and index.
   ISBN 1-55591-265-6 (pbk.)
     1. Hispanic Americans—History. 2. United States—Civilization—Hispanic influences. 3. Hispanic Americans and mass media. I. Title.
E184.S75K38   1998
973'.0468—dc21   98-10146
                            CIP

Fulcrum Publishing
350 Indiana Street, Suite 350
Golden, Colorado 80401-5093
(800) 992-2908 • (303) 277-1623
e-mail: fulcrum@fulcrum-books.com
website: www.fulcrum-books.com

For Crissy and Miguel with love
Para mi esposa Cristelia Pérez y mi hijo
Miguel José con cariño

Contents

Introduction

Hispanic peoples have lived in and developed their civilization in North America, including areas that later became part of the United States, since before the landing of the *Mayflower*. And before Columbus's ships and the *Mayflower* landed, competition between two of the greatest European empires predisposed competition and conflict in the Western Hemisphere between the Anglo-Saxon, English-speaking and the mixed-race, Spanish-speaking peoples. This competition and conflict has characterized Anglo and Hispanic relations not only in the hemisphere but also within the United States specifically since the beginning of the American Republic. More importantly for this book, the image of Hispanic peoples of the United States has been cast through a prism created by ideologies and government policies that furthered preexisting misconceptions and created others regarding the nature of Hispanics in the hemisphere and within the borders of the United States. This prejudice, or "Hispanophobia," has been pervasive and consistent throughout U.S. history and into the present:

> Our national habit of condescension and oversimplification of virtually all phenomena of the Hispanic world is a habit that stretches from our elementary schools to universities to the White House, and it grows out of ancestral antagonisms that have come to constitute a perennial prejudice as unjustifiable as it can be dangerous. The very depth of this prejudice renders it difficult

to discern, especially when camouflaged by relatively superficial immediacies—such as, for example, an Argentine political crisis, a Guatemalan revolution, a Bay of Pigs episode, and the kidnapping of an ambassador. It is a prejudice that defies correction, because it is pervasive among so many of the teachers, writers, and politicians who guide our attitudes concerning Hispanic countries and their relationships to us. (Powell, 4)

Two ideologies help us to understand the role that was cast for the future Hispanic residents of the United States: the Spanish Black Legend and Manifest Destiny. These ideologies and their premises were to play important roles in the fashioning of government policies on immigration, education, employment, and welfare. They are policies and programs very much relevant to U.S. Hispanic citizens today and, while continuing to influence the definition of U.S. Hispanics as a group, are still troubling to the national conscience. They are policies and programs that are still hotly debated and rapidly evolving, even at this book's publication.

The cultural, and at times even bellicose, conflict of Hispanic and Anglo-Saxon peoples within the expanding U.S. empire during the nineteenth and twentieth centuries is to a significant degree an expression of the Anglo-Saxon desire for hegemony over other peoples. Anglo-American relations with Hispanics in and outside of the borders of the United States have been characterized by the creation of doctrines that make possible the subjugation of Hispanics by Anglos. Among the most important sets of these doctrines are those known as Manifest Destiny and the Monroe Doctrine. At each step in the expansion of the American Republic, these ideological doctrines have made possible the acquisition of lands, technologies, and human resources—especially manual and skilled labor—by the United

States, while limiting competition for the same from extra-hemispheric interests. At each step in the evolution of the American Republic, popular and academic culture have fashioned images of Hispanics to correspond to and facilitate their economic and political exploitation. Whereas the republics of Hispanic America have seen their self-determination and even some of their lands and peoples swallowed up by the monster to the north, it has been the Hispanics who live within the United States that have felt the most direct and constant impact of the images fashioned through governmental decisions and policy—decisions made in compliance with the industries that have greatly benefited from the exploitation of Hispanic labor, lands, and resources. Much of this exploitation has been facilitated by furthering stereotypes of Hispanics through education and the popular media.

It is the purpose of this book to chronicle and analyze the changing images of Hispanics in the United States from the period of exploration and conquest to the present, when once again Hispanics have risen to become significant populations in some of the regions where they once predominated: Florida and the Southwest. But the large concentrations of Hispanics in the Northeast and the Midwest have also resulted in measurable part from U.S. political and economic hegemony over lands once claimed by Spain: Mexico and the Spanish-speaking islands of the Caribbean.

Before entering into the discussion of the evolution of the images that Anglo-American society has fashioned for Hispanics, I will briefly review in Chapter One: A Hidden Legacy the considerable contributions that Hispanics have made to the building of U.S. society and culture; it is a tale that should be all too familiar to us as a society but has somehow continued to slip from focus in both education and popular culture. After that, I shall discuss how The Spanish Black Legend was fashioned to facilitate European expansion into the New World, and how that blended with the doctrine of Manifest Destiny to produce the media images that are still very much with us today. In all, it should be remembered that while A Hidden Legacy represents a history that is resonant with how Hispanics often see themselves, the latter part of the chapter concentrates on the evolution of how Hispanics have been characterized in Anglo-American intellectual history and popular culture. It is precisely this Anglo-American image of Hispanics that has continued to influence current history, popular culture, news gathering, and the formulation of social policy that affects Hispanics around the country as well as abroad.

Chapter One

A HIDDEN LEGACY

IT IS A RARE HISTORY BOOK OF THE UNITED STATES that begins by describing the introduction of Western civilization *by Hispanics* to the lands and cultural patrimony that eventually would belong to the United States. In addition to a realistic appraisal of the great and lasting contributions of Native Americans to what would become the United States, the evaluation and integration into our official national history of the Hispanic contribution is long overdue. Its absence and/or minimalization is a heinous intellectual crime because, in fact, many of the institutions and values that have been so trumpeted as Anglo-American were really first introduced by Hispanic peoples—Spaniards, Hispanicized Africans and Amerindians, mestizos, and mulattos. Not only were advanced technologies, such as those essential to ranching and mining, introduced by the Hispanics, so were all of the values and perspectives inherent in Western intellectual culture—regardless of positive or negative worth or whether for ultimate good or ill in the long run. For better or worse, Spain was the first disseminator in the New World of Western civilization, and even its mixed-breed children have continued to blend that tradition with that of the

1

indigenous peoples of the Americas and the peoples imported from Africa for five hundred years.

THE WRITTEN WORD AND EDUCATION

It was the Spanish-speaking peoples who first introduced and furthered European-style literacy and literate culture, not only in the hemisphere, but also in what would become the continental United States. The first introduction of a written European language into an area that would become the mainland United States was accomplished in Florida by Juan Ponce de León in 1513 with his travel diaries; but in U.S. popular and educational culture, Ponce de León is instead wrongly memorialized for his mythic folly of searching for a fountain of youth. From Ponce de León on, the history of literacy, books, and writing in what was to become the United States is developed by Spanish, Hispanicized Africans and Amerindians, and mestizo and mulatto missionaries, soldiers, and settlers. Later, the English, Dutch, and French would continue this introduction of European culture when they began to colonize more northerly regions of North America. Ponce de León's exploration marks the beginning of keeping civil, military, and ecclesiastical records that would eventually become commonplace in the Hispanic South and Southwest of what would become the United States.[1]

The value and transcendency of written culture's introduction as understood by the Western world is inestimable. It not only facilitated keeping records of conquest and colonization, maintaining correspondence, planting the rudiments of commerce, and standardizing social organization, it also gave birth to the first written descriptions and studies of the fauna and flora of these lands new to the Europeans and mestizos, made possible the writing of laws for

2

governance and commercial exploitation, and for writing and maintaining a history—an official story and tradition—of Hispanic culture in these lands.

Of course, this introduction of writing in the Spanish language was followed by the importation of books, first authorized to Mexico in 1525, very shortly after Hernán Cortés's conquest of the Aztecs. Thereafter, the printing press was introduced in Mexico City by Juan Pablos (Giovanni Paoli) in 1539, and by the end of the sixteenth century there were already some nine presses functioning in the capital of New Spain. (García Izcabalceta) This was followed by the publication of newspapers by Juan Pablos's press beginning in 1541. (Garner, 3–5)

What may be surprising to many readers is that printing by Hispanics in the Northeast, principally in New York City and Philadelphia, dates back to the 1790s and that publishing books in Spanish there began in the following decade. Numerous publishing houses issued not only political and commercial books but original, creative literature written principally by Cubans and Spaniards. To date, the earliest Spanish-language newspapers that have been documented in what became the United States were *El Misisipi* in New Orleans in 1808, *La Gaceta de Texas,* and *El Mexicano* in 1813 in Nacogdoches, Texas/ Natchitoshes, Louisiana. New York's first Spanish-language newspaper, *El Mensajero Semanal,* was founded in 1828.[2] Throughout the nineteenth century, despite the existence of Spanish-language publishers and printers, the principal publishers of Spanish literature and all types of information in the United States and northern Mexico (most of the West and Southwest as we know it today) were the hundreds of newspapers that existed from New York to New Orleans, Taos, and San Francisco. Literally

3

hundreds of newspapers carried news of commerce and politics as well as poetry, serialized novels, stories, essays, and opinion, both from the pens of local writers as well as from the most highly regarded writers and intellectuals of the entire Hispanic world, from Spain to Argentina. And when northern Mexico and Louisiana were incorporated into the United States, this journalistic and intellectual discourse, rather than abate, intensified. The newspapers took on the task of preserving the Spanish language and Hispanic culture in territories and states where Hispanic residents were becoming rapidly and vastly outnumbered by Anglo and European migrants— or pioneers, if you prefer, although they were hardly pioneers if both Hispanics and Amerindians had already lived there and established institutions in those areas. The newspapers became forums for discussions of rights, both cultural and civil, they became the libraries and memories of the small towns in New Mexico, the *"defensores de la raza"* (defenders of Hispanic civil rights) in the large cities, and quite often they were the only Spanish-language textbook for learning to read and write Spanish— and they were excellent textbooks at that. Many of the more successful newspapers grew into publishing houses at the end of the nineteenth century and the beginning of the twentieth.

Of all of the major centers of Hispanic culture in the United States, from San Francisco to Tampa and New York, it was San Antonio that received the strongest community of expatriate intellectuals from the Mexican Revolution. The city maintained more than a dozen publishing houses during the 1920s, accounting for the greatest flourishing of printed discourse and art that Hispanic communities have ever experienced in the United States.

All of the institutions—schools; universities; libraries; state, county, and municipal archives; courts; and almost an infinity of others—that are common fundaments of today's advanced social organization, science, and technology, and that so rely on literate culture, were first introduced to North America by Hispanics. The first universities in the hemisphere were St. Thomas Aquinas in Santo Domingo, founded in 1538, and the Universities of Mexico and San Marcos in Lima, both founded in 1551. All three are still functioning today, but St. Thomas under a new name: the Authonomous University of Santo Domingo. During the colonial period, Spain founded some twenty-six universities in the Americas in addition to numerous theological seminaries. In colonial times, the universities followed the general models of the Universities of Salamanca and Alcalá de Henares in Spain, offering studies in humanities, theology, law, and medicine. Latin was the official language used in classes, although some universities taught the indigenous languages for a while. Later, they also taught mathematics and physics. The degrees that were offered were the bachelors, masters (or licentiate), and doctorate.

The Jesuits were the most important teaching order in the Americas. During the seventeenth century, the University of Mexico achieved the greatest distinction in the Americas, boasting twenty-three chairs, most of which were in canon law and theology, but with others in medicine, surgery, anatomy, astrology, rhetoric, and the Aztec and Otomí languages. In the last quarter of the seventeenth century, the university also held the distinction of serving as home for the greatest intellectual of the period: the mathematician and historian Carlos de Sigüenza y Góngora (1645–1700). In 1693, this scholar, in the tradition of the Renaissance man, accompanied Admiral Andrés de Pez on a scientific

5

expedition into what is today the southeastern United Sates to study the local topography, fauna, and flora. He later published his findings in Mexico City, becoming the first scientist and university professor in the world to have studied the flora and fauna of Texas and what would become the Gulf Coast states of the United States. He entitled his book *Description de la bahía de Santa María de Galve (antes Penzacola), de la Movila o Mississippi, en la costa septentrional del seno mejicano* (Description of the Bay of Santa María de Galve [previously Penzacola], of Mobile or Mississippi, on the Eastern Coast of the Gulf of Mexico). In addition to his book about the lands around the northeastern Gulf of Mexico, he also published *Historia de la provincia de Tejas* (History of the Province of Texas). Sigüenza y Góngora authored numerous other books in all the fields of his broad interests and also had the distinction of publishing the first newspaper in Mexico: *El Mercurio Volante* (Winged Mercury). Finally, his encyclopedic knowledge and study extended to include what might be considered anthropology today. He researched and wrote about Aztecs and the Chichimecas in his books *Genealogía de los reyes mejicanos* (Genealogy of the Mexican Kings) and *Historia del imperio de los chichimecas* (History of the Chichimeca Empire). Sigüenza y Góngora died in 1700 in Mexico City. Unfortunately, a devastating fire in Mexico City in 1792 consumed many of his manuscripts. (Fontana, 77; Kanellos and Pérez, 1995, 44, 49)

The first schools in what would become the continental United States were established by 1600 in Spanish Catholic missions in what are today Florida, Georgia, and New Mexico. Actually, the first elementary school established in the Americas was opened in Santo Domingo in 1505 for the children of the Spaniards. From then on, elementary schools were included in convents, where children were taught reading, writing, arithmetic, and religion. Later, the mission system in the Americas functioned to instruct the children of Indians and mestizos. (Kanellos and Pérez, 1995, 24) The first school in an area that would become part of the United States was established in 1513: the Escuela de Gramática (Grammar School) in Puerto Rico, which was opened at the Cathedral of San Juan by Bishop Alonso Manso. The Escuela de Gramática served as a free secondary school in which Latin language and literature, history, science, art, philosophy, and theology were taught. Shortly after the founding of the Escuela de Gramática primary education was offered at schools connected to churches on the island. (Kanellos and Pérez, 1995, 30; Dolan and Deck, 296)

The first attempts at creating public schools in what would become the U.S. Southwest occurred in Texas and California. As elsewhere in the Spanish colonies, education was offered in the missions. Not only was it important for the children of the settlers to learn to read, write, and master arithmetic, but the mission education system most importantly fostered the religious conversion and acculturation of the Amerindians, as well as their conversion into a laboring class that received food, clothes, and protection for their servitude.[3]

The first person to translate books from a European language (Spanish) into an Indian language in what would become the United States was the Franciscan missionary Francisco Pareja. Brother Pareja translated the books into the Timicuan language from about 1612 to 1627 in what is now the state of Georgia. As early as 1513, the king of Spain had issued an edict ordering that Latin be taught to select Indians. After that, schools for Indians developed and became important, especially in Mexico and Peru where, in

7

addition to Latin and religion, painting, sculpture, and other trades were taught. As regards the Amerindian populations of the New World—and especially what became the West and Southwest of the United States—despite atrocities committed by Spanish soldiers and colonists, it was Spain and the Catholic Church that recognized Native Americans as human beings. They sought to bring the Amerindians into their religion and their interpretation of the universe, rather than eliminating them or forcing their reduced numbers off their lands and into reservations.

In 1509, Pope Julius II authorized the Catholic kings of Spain to administer the Catholic Church in the Americas in exchange for underwriting the costs of evangelization of the New World. It was largely because of this acceptance of the Native Americans' humanity that Hispanic America is today predominantly populated by mestizos—descendants of mixed Spanish and Native American blood. The mission education system was central to the very creation and rise of the mestizo population of the Americas, including the Southwest of the United States.

The first effort to provide a public school outside of the walls of missions took place in 1746 in Béxar (today's San Antonio, Texas) in an effort to provide religious education to the children of the Villa of San Fernando. Unfortunately, this school was short lived. (Chipman, 256) While schooling at missions was firmly established throughout the Spanish colonies, public education was not consistently promoted until almost the nineteenth century. The king of Spain first mandated public education in the Spanish colonies in 1793. High illiteracy among soldiers prompted the king to issue the mandate. But the implementation of the mandate did not reach the far northern provinces of California, for example, until the 1800s. (Kanellos, 1990, 291) The first public schools in California were established in

1794 under orders of Spanish Governor Diego de Borica. Ten schools in five different cities were built during his term from 1794 to 1800. Successive governors established more schools during their terms; nevertheless, most of the schools established during the Spanish period failed. Among the many reasons for their defeat were the lack of a public education tradition among the settlers, the isolation and sparseness of the population, general indifference, and financial problems. Despite these frustrated efforts, there were some landmarks in the history of education. For instance, in 1802 the Spanish governor of Texas, Juan Bautista Elguezábal, issued the first compulsory school attendance law for children up to age twelve, stipulating heavy fines for parents who did not comply. Thus in the Southwest, the tradition of free, compulsory education up to a certain age dates back to this effort in Texas. (Chipman, 257; Kanellos, 1990, 291–292) On the whole, the populations on the northern frontier fared better during the Mexican period of government, when the missions were secularized and the responsibility for education shifted into the hands of a liberal government struggling to establish a democracy. (Kanellos, 1990, 292)

SCIENCE, TECHNOLOGY, AND INDUSTRY

There are no official American history books that really document that the building of the first European-style towns and cities, the first ports for commerce, the introduction of the first European-bred livestock, the first ranching, the first mining, the first roads and highways, the first civil engineering, the introduction of technologies from Europe—much of this complex of technology and development in vast areas that became the United States should be credited to the Spaniards and their mixed-blood descendants. Many important agricultural products were first introduced by

Hispanics: the farming of wheat, cotton, and wine grapes; the breeding and tending of livestock. What is conveniently ignored or sidestepped in history books and intellectual discussion of the development of "civilization" in the United States is the priority of Hispanic intellectual, scientific, and technological advances in North America, very large components of the making of our nation. These advances include the Spanish-mestizo accomplishments in settling large portions of what would become the United States.

Rightly speaking, the oldest colonies of today's United States were not the thirteen colonies, but Puerto Rico and the Virgin Islands—we must own up to our responsibility as a colonial power, an empire, in possession of these two colonies—as well as other former Spanish colonies that passed to the United States, such as Guam. And rightly speaking, some of the first educational, religious, and government institutions that have survived in the United States first existed on the island of Puerto Rico. Puerto Rico has the distinction of being the oldest colony in the hemisphere: a

Columbus taking leave of the Catholic monarchs.
Courtesy Library of Congress.

colony of Spain from 1493 to 1898, and since 1898 a colony of the United States. In religious organization, Puerto Rico has the distinction of not only being the oldest diocese in the United States but of the entire New World. In 1511, Pope Julius II established the Diocese of San Juan Bautista and named the first bishop in the hemisphere, Alonso Manso.

Included in the costly feats of major European exploration of the North American continent were Antonio de Alaminos's discovery in 1513 of the Gulf Stream (a discovery that resulted in Florida becoming a strategic stopping place for voyages); Alvarez de Pineda's exploration of the Gulf of Mexico and his claiming Texas for Spain in 1519; Alvar Núñez Cabeza de Vaca's travels through the South and Southwest of what would become the United States from 1528 to 1536; Her-

City Gate, St. Augustine.
Courtesy Library of Congress.

nando de Soto's exploration from 1539 to 1542 of what would become Florida, Alabama, Mississippi, Tennessee, North Carolina, Arkansas, and Louisiana, and his discovery of the Mississippi River; Francisco Vásquez de Coronado's encounter with the Grand Canyon, the Rio Grande River, and numerous Indian nations in the Southwest in 1540 as well as his ventures as far north as today's state of Nebraska; Pedro Menéndez de Avilés's contribution in the sixteenth century to designing and developing the shipping routes and drawing up regulations for trade in the West

11

Indies; Esteban Gómez's voyage in 1524–1525 up the North American coast from Florida to the present-day state of Maine, venturing into Hudson Bay and the Delaware and Connecticut Rivers some eighty years before Henry Hudson; Juan Rodríguez de Cabrillo's voyage of 1542 up the Pacific coast into San Diego Bay, thus beginning the exploration of Alta California; Juan de Fuca's exploration in 1590 of the Pacific coast to the present-day state of Washington (Spanish maps of the period show the Strait of Juan de Fuca as a possible Northwest Passage); Juan de Oñate and his expedition's colonization of New Mexico in 1598; Spanish expeditions in 1773 exploring the Pacific coast of Canada all the way up to Alaska, establishing a base at Nootka on the coast of Vancouver Island; Pedro de Garcés, a Franciscan missionary, founding in 1774 the first overland route to California; Spanish ships exploring from 1790 to 1792 the northern reaches of North America, mapping out portions of Canada and Alaska, and starting short-lived settlements such as those in Valdez and Córdoba.

The majority of these feats of exploration, facilitated by the most advanced maritime technology and navigational science of the time, opened up these North American lands for colonization. Vásquez de Coronado, for example, reported to the king of Spain that he had found lands poor in metals but rich in livestock and very suitable for farming; this led to Juan de Oñate's colony becoming established in New Mexico in 1598. Earlier than that, in 1560, the Spanish had founded Santa Elena in what is today the state of South Carolina, the first European settlement in what became the continental United States. Both Santa Elena and later St. Augustine, founded in 1565, predate Jamestown, which was not founded by the English until 1607; they also predate the arrival of the *Mayflower* at Plymouth in 1620. By 1573, the Franciscan Order had arrived in Florida to

12

establish missions, which a century later would extend along the east coast of North America from St. Augustine, Florida, to North Carolina. The Franciscans also established a string of missions from St. Augustine westward to present-day Tennessee. Theirs was also the first mission in Texas, San Francisco de los Tejas, founded by Fathers Massanet and Fontcubierta

Fort San Carlos, Penzacola, Florida. Courtesy Library of Congress.

near the Neches River in 1690—it was later moved to San Antonio. Another eight missions among the Indian nations were soon authorized for Texas, spanning from east Texas to San

A presidio soldier. Courtesy Library of Congress.

Antonio and Goliad, including the still-standing and famous San Antonio missions: San Antonio Valero, San Juan Capistrano, San Francisco de la Espada, and La Purísima Concepción Mission. In 1731, fifteen families (fifty-six people) from the Canary Islands arrived to colonize what would later become the city of San Antonio, Texas. They called their first civil settlement San Fernando de Bexar, which is still reflected today in the name of Bejar County.

In 1691, Jesuit Father Eusebio Kino began his string of missions in Arizona, which would grow to include San Xavier del Bac near Tucson as well as the following: Nuestra Señora de los Dolores, Santa Gertrudis de Saric, San José de Imuris, Nuestra Señora de los Remedios, and San Cayetano de Tumacácori. In 1761, José de Gálvez brought the first colonists into San Diego Bay, Alta California, and, by 1769, Father Junípero Serra began establishing his string of missions along almost

Junípero Serra.
Courtesy Library of Congress.

the entire length of California. He eventually founded ten missions, traveled more than ten thousand miles, and converted close to six thousand eight hundred Amerindians. Father Serra's death in 1823 did not stop his missionary activity in California; his fellow Franciscans established another twelve missions. Thus, by 1823, the famous mission trail of California included San Diego de Alcalá (1769); San Carlos de Monterrey (1770); San Antonio de

14

Padua Mission (1771); San Gabriel Arcángel (1771); San Luis Obispo de Tolosa (1772); San Francisco de Asís (1776); San Juan Capistrano (1776); Santa Clara de Asís (1777); San Buenaventura (1782); Santa Bárbara (1786); La Purísima Concepción (1787); Santa Cruz (1791); San José de Guadalupe (1797); San Juan Bautista (1797); San Miguel Arcángel (1797); San Fernando Rey (1797); San Luis Rey (1798); Santa Inés (1804); San Rafael Arcángel (1817); and San Francisco

San Antonio's San José y San Miguel Aguayo Mission. Courtesy Library of Congress.

Solano (1823). By 1766, the presidio San Francisco was established. The cities of San Francisco, San José, and Los Angeles were founded in 1776, 1777, and 1781 respectively.

San Luis Rey Mission, Oceanside, California. Courtesy Library of Congress.

The missions throughout the Southwest and South—as well as in all of New Spain—were the basis for a European-style social organization, the education of the Natives, the creation of a self-supporting economic base through the development of local industry, and the foun-

Santa Barbara Mission.
Courtesy Library of Congress.

dation laying that would eventually become a network of towns, cities, and commerce. Many areas in the southern and southwestern United States still have the Spanish names given by their founders, have their cities laid out in the grids created by those colonizers, have paved highways over the roads and paths blazed by these colonists, and even derive livelihoods from industries intro-

Fachada de la Mision de San Xavier del Bac, Tucson, Arizona.
Courtesy Library of Congress.

duced or developed by the early Hispanics.

St. Augustine bears the distinction of being the oldest permanent European settlement in the continental United States. It became the most important strategic post for the Spaniards in defending the Florida coast—the only one that endured storms, fires, famine, and raids by Indians and the French and English. During the seventeenth century, St. Augustine and other areas of Florida received considerable migration from Spain and the Spanish Caribbean. But in 1763, the region of the Florida Peninsula called East Florida—as opposed to West Florida, which ranged from the Georgia Coast to the Mississippi River—came under British control as a result of the Treaty of Paris. This included St. Augustine. In 1783, under the Treaty of Versailles, East Florida was returned to Spain and remained so until 1821, when it was surrendered to the United States. Louisiana, which had been "discovered," charted, and claimed by the Spanish but settled in part by the French from Canada, remained a French colony until 1763, when it, too, passed back into Spanish possession as a result of the Treaty of Paris. Louisiana was ceded to France in 1801 but was sold to the United States by Napoleon in 1803.

All of the feats of Hispanic exploration were the result of advances in various sciences and technologies, most obvious of which were navigation and cartography, but also included many others. The results of exploration necessitated further pioneering efforts in shipping, transportation, architecture, and city planning. In fact, European-style architecture was initiated in the hemisphere a century before the landing at Plymouth Rock with the construction of the San Nicolás de Bari Church in the city of Santo Domingo from 1503 to 1508. In 1512, the first hospital was also constructed in Santo Domingo. The Spanish-Amerindian built presidios (forts) and missions were the first European-style architectural works introduced into what would become the United States, from Florida to California. Many of them survive and function to this date and are still highly regarded for their grace and beauty as well as their adaptation to the environment. Many of the missions of the Southwest in fact are regarded as important works of art. The houses built by the settlers and soldiers were the first examples of European- and mestizo-style civil architecture in these lands, as were their aqueducts, presidios, government buildings, and other constructions.

Missionaries, explorers, and naturalists studied the native flora and fauna and wrote and drew meticulous descriptions of nature and the native civilizations. They may be considered early ethnographers, anthropologists, linguists, botanists, and pioneers of other social and natural sciences. One of the best examples of this pioneering ethnographic work was Alvar Núñez Cabeza de Vaca's *The Account*, published in 1542, which described in detail the customs of the Native populations all along the Gulf Coast of what would become the United States. Even the customs of the far-off Alaska Natives were first studied by Hispanics. As early as 1792, naturalist José Mariano Moziño Suárez Losada, on an expedition led by Juan Bodega y Cuadra, was the first to study and describe the Nootka region of Alaska, leaving for posterity detailed written accounts of the Native inhabitants. His companion, artist Atanasio Echeverría y Godoy, became the first to depict the plants, animals, people, and scenes in the Nootka region. (Fontana, 186) Another example of this early work was penned in 1693 by the great humanist and scientist of the University of Mexico, Carlos de Sigüenza y Góngora, who has been noted earlier.

The Spanish, mestizo, and Hispanicized Indians and Africans who first settled in the lands from Florida to California were responsible for introducing and creating many industries that would flourish under U.S. rule. They established the bases for the agriculture and mining that would especially dominate the economies of the southwestern United States. By 1600, the Spanish settlers along the Rio Grande Valley had introduced the plow and beasts of burden to the Indians, thus revolutionizing agricultural technology that would endure for centuries in what would become the American Southwest. They also introduced irrigation and new craft techniques, such as those involved in carpentry and blacksmithing, and a new profit-driven economy. (Fontana, 80–81) In 1610, the first irrigation canals and irrigation systems north of the Rio Grande were built in Santa Fe, New Mexico, by Spanish, Indian, and mestizo colonizers. They dug two *acequias madres* (main ditches) on each side of the small river that passed through the center of the town they were establishing. The Spanish had strict codes and plans for the construction of irrigation systems for the towns they were founding in the arid Southwest; such systems were constructed often in advance of the building of forts, houses, and churches. The undertaking was quite often massive, calling for the digging, dredging, and transportation of materials and feeding of humans and animals. This was the case in the founding of Albuquerque in 1706, of San Antonio in 1731, and of Los Angeles in 1781. The canals of San Antonio were so well planned, lined with stone and masonry as they were, that many of them are still functioning today. (Simmons, 138–139; Meyer, 37–41)

The foundation that was laid for farming and agriculture has resulted in California, Texas, and Florida being the largest producers of fruits and vegetables in the world.

Sugar

Paramount among the agricultural products that the Spaniards introduced to the hemisphere was sugar: white gold. Sugarcane was introduced to the New World by Columbus during his second voyage in 1493. Originally from India, the plant was taken first to Hispaniola and then to the rest of the Americas for its cultivation. The first sugar mill was built in 1508 or 1509 on Hispaniola, the current island home of the Dominican Republic and Haiti, and the first samples of sugar were sent to Spain about 1515. By 1523, there were twenty-four mills operating on the island. All of the technology, plants, and technicians involved in sugar production were first brought to the New World by the Spaniards. (Mintz, 117) Among the technological advances in the industry was the development of a more efficient and rapid sugar mill in either Mexico or Peru around the year 1600; it was later disseminated throughout the Americas engaged in sugar production. It was the vertical three-roller mill, which allowed for a quicker and more thorough extraction of the sugar juice.

Sugar has had much to do with the development of Hispanic culture in the United States. Beginning with illicit trade between the British colonies and Cuba, and lasting well into the twentieth century, Anglo-America came to depend on Caribbean sugar—as did much of the world—until sugar beets were grown and protected as a crop in the United States. (Mintz, 120) Between 1838 and 1860, Cuba was the world's largest producer of sugar. In 1850, sugar accounted for 83 percent of Cuban exports, most of which came to the United States. By 1860, the island was producing one-half million tons per year. (Kanellos and Pérez, 1995, 91) The importance of sugar coincided with U.S. overtures to purchase Cuba from Spain, as will be discussed in later chapters.

Cigar Manufacturing

Another industry, which was at first based in the Caribbean but later was transplanted to the United States, was that of cigar making. Cuba was the acknowledged world leader in the creation of the industry that would have millions of males in the United States at the end of the nineteenth century conspicuously advertising their business success and affluence by puffing on the large odorous cylinders. In fact, the development of one of the major cities in the United States is related to the first transfer of a whole industry from Latin America to the States and the building of a company town. This transplant began in 1886, when Spanish and Cuban entrepreneurs acquired Florida swampland near Tampa and built a cigar-producing town, Ybor City. In 1880, the population of Tampa was only 721; a decade later the combined population of Tampa and Ybor City was five thousand five hundred, and that number tripled by 1900.

The first of the entrepreneurs to establish their own cigar factories, Vicente Martínez Ybor and Ignacio Haya, hoped to attract a docile workforce—unlike the labor union activists in Cuba—avoid U.S. import tariffs, and get closer to their markets in the United States. Also, the Cuban wars for independence were raging and continually disrupting business. The industry in Ybor City grew to ten factories by 1895 and became the principal cigar-producing area in the United States, when smoking cigars was at its highest peak. (Henderson and Mormino, 40–45, 262)

Cattle, Livestock Industries, and Related Fields

The Spanish introduced European livestock into North America and the entire hemisphere. Both the reintroduction of the horse into the Americas and the importation of cattle became the foundation for the all-important cattle industry. Spanish conquistadores Hernán Cortés and Gregorio Villalobos introduced ranching to Mexico in 1521 with the importation from Cuba of cattle for breeding purposes. This was the beginning of the ranching industry and culture on the mainland that would travel north and eventually become one of the principal industries of the American Southwest, and later the West and Midwest. Not only were cattle introduced, but also all of the macroorganic components of ranch ecology, which included cattle, sheep, goats, hogs, and the plant species these animals consume. (Bennett and Hoffmann, 90–95) Also by 1521, Spanish explorers had taken horses and cattle to Florida on Juan Ponce de León's second trip. Hernando de Soto was next to import livestock to Florida, including more than three hundred horses and some cattle in 1539.

It was in what is now Florida that the Spanish established the first stock raising; missions spearheaded settlement and stock raising. By 1565, some stock raising was established around St. Augustine and Tallahassee, with the first ranchers raising cattle for local consumption and also for smuggling stock to Cuba. However, ranching was difficult in the swamps and tropics; it was unable to develop as it later did in California and Texas. (Slatta, 10) Nevertheless, the first large and successful ranches in what would become the United States developed and flourished in Florida much before ranching became profitable in Texas and California.

In 1663, Florida-born Tomás Menéndez Márquez inherited his deceased father's cattle ranch in central Florida and built it up over the years into the largest ranch and provider of hides, dried meat, and tallow to the Spanish settlements in Florida and for export through shipping to Havana via the Florida port of San Martín. Menéndez Márquez owned his own frigate, which he used to transport his own goods along with chartered freight to market in Havana; he would return to Florida with extensive trade items to be sold. His business interests expanded into areas far beyond ranching, including the importation of Cuban rum. His fortunes increased further when, in 1684, he was appointed royal *contador,* or accountant/treasurer, for Florida. His La Chúa Ranch became the largest cattle ranch on lands that would become the United States, extending from the St. Johns River westward to the Gulf and from Lake George northward to the Santa Fe River. Within its boundaries was contained what are today Ocala, Payne's Prairie, Alachua, Palatka, and Gainesville. The ranch produced more than one-third of Florida's cattle and horses in the late seventeenth century. The ranch met its end, however, when in 1702 James Moore led Carolinians and Creek Indians into the Florida Peninsula and overran La Chúa, causing the ranch hands to flee and the cattle to become feral. (Henderson and Mormino, 118–139)

Cattle and ranching were first introduced north of the Rio Grande River in 1598 by Spanish-Mexican colonists headed by Juan de Oñate when they crossed the river with seven thousand head of cattle somewhere near present-day El Paso into what became New Mexico. Besides cattle, Oñate brought in more than four thousand head of shaggy sheep, which became the foundation of the modern Navajo-*churro* breed. The first ranches along the Rio Grande in Texas were founded from 1659 to 1682. The lead Spanish colonizer and

Hacienda owner. Courtesy Library of Congress.

future governor of the Province of New Mexico, Oñate, established a livestock industry that would supply the burgeoning silver mining industry in northern New Spain, especially around Zacatecas and Guanajuato. There was an intense demand for cattle, horses, and mules as well as for tallow for candles, hides for water, and ore bags, clothing, harnesses, hinges, and numerous other items. From New Mexico and western Texas, cattle and livestock ranching spread into the Great Plains, and became the basis of much of the livestock industry of today.

In 1687, Father Eusebio Kino established the mission of Nuestra Señora de los Dolores in Arizona, through which he introduced livestock to the Pimería Alta region of southern Arizona and northern Sonora. At this and at least twenty other locations in Arizona Kino introduced and promoted livestock tending as essential in converting and feeding the Pima Indians. Franciscan missionaries continued to spread ranching and livestock tending throughout missions in Arizona, New Mexico, and California. (Slatta, 22) In Arizona, as elsewhere in the Southwest, land grants to early settlers and soldiers became cattle ranches. A small farm land grant in

Frederick Remington's depiction of vaqueros. *Courtesy Library of Congress.*

Tubac, Arizona, received from Spain in 1789 by Toribio Otero became the basis generations later for the making of "the cattle king of Tubac": his great grandson Sabino Otero. On the basis of this initial inherited ranch, Sabino Otero built the largest ranching operation in southern Arizona during the 1870s and 1880s. (Sheridan, 51–53)

In 1690, an expedition headed by Captain Alonso de León brought livestock to the first Spanish mission in east Texas: San Francisco de los Tejas. This was the beginning of the cattle industry in east Texas, as this and other missions continued to be stocked as well as to raise their own livestock. (Slatta, 21) In 1721, the Marquis of San Miguel de Aguayo laid the ground for ranching along the northern bank of the Rio Grande River when he brought four hundred sheep and three hundred cattle into South Texas from Nuevo León. Around 1722, he also introduced large numbers of horses, mules, cattle, and sheep to be ranched at the missions in the San Antonio area. In 1748, José Escandón brought four thousand colonists into the area, and the expanded population base made livestock raising even more important. In 1757, one José de la Tienda reported more than eighty thousand head of cattle, horses, and mules, and more than three hundred thousand sheep and goats in the area. In 1760, Captain Blas María de la Garza Falcón obtained a grant to 975,000 acres of land in Texas, which he called Rancho Real de Santa Petronila. That ranch in time would become the largest cattle ranch in the United States and the world: the King Ranch. (Kanellos and Pérez, 1995, 57) By 1781, nearly all available land grants in South Texas had been assigned and nearly all were in use as ranches. (Simons and Hoyt, 60; Chipman, 246–247)

Around 1750, the Spanish governor of Texas attempted in vain to license and regulate the illegal trade in cattle between Spanish Texas and French Louisiana: these were the first cattle drives on record. *Vaqueros,* Hispanic cowboys, had been illegally driving cattle from Texas to market in French Louisiana for decades. When Spain acquired Louisiana in 1763, this trade was no longer illegal; however, when the Louisiana Territory passed to the United States in 1803, cattle driving from Texas to Louisiana once again constituted a lucrative smuggling trade. By the late eighteenth century, some fifteen to twenty thousand head of cattle moved eastward to Louisiana each year. By the early 1800s, illegal horse and mule trading also became a lucrative business, and Anglo settlers in the Mississippi Valley provided an expanded market for all Texas livestock. (Slatta, 19, 22) By the eighteenth century, the first major livestock economies were flourishing in Texas: horse ranching in Nacogdoches, cattle and horse ranching along the Rio Grande Valley and around San Antonio and south to La Bahía. Cattle ran free on the open range and were herded and driven to market and slaughter. According to Slatta, the Anglo immigrants who settled in Texas considered these cattle "wild" and simply appropriated them, although they belonged to the Hispanic ranchers and were tended by *vaqueros.* They considered the cattle to be open game. They did not create a cattle industry, they simply took it over. (Slatta, 19; Bennett and Hoffman, 98–100)

Also around the 1830s, the first longhorn cattle appeared, resulting from the crossbreeding of the Spanish retintos and animals brought to Texas by Anglo settlers. Immune to tick fever and accustomed to the tough brush country of South Texas, the Longhorn became the basis for the western livestock industry. Texas beef was poised to become an important industry for the United States on the eve of Texas independence. (Slatta, 19) After the American Civil War,

26

cattle ranching became especially important to the nation; Texas cowboys drove some ten million heads of longhorn north to railroad heads and markets. Over time, the long-horn was replaced by many other breeds, but in the initial stages of this important industry it became the mainstay. Along with the trade in beef, an industry in hides, tallow, and other by-products flourished in coastal "factories" of Texas. (Slatta, 19–20)

Cattle ranching was first introduced to California in 1769 by the Franciscan missionary, Father Junípero Serra, with the founding of the mission at San Diego. He proceeded to establish missions and their reliance on livestock tending, ranching, and farming all along the California coast. The missions became the largest landholders in California and taught the skills of ranching, raising livestock, and farming European crops to the neophyte Indians they converted. The Indians lived in conditions similar to Medieval serfs in exchange for the food, clothing, and protection offered by the missionaries, who were supposed to be holding the Indians' communal lands for them until they could assume the respon-sibility themselves. With this cheap labor, the missions grew into the greatest trading and landholding power in Califor-nia. They began to accumulate wealth as a result of the con-siderable trade conducted not only with the civilian and military populations of California, but with traders who came by sea from as far away as Boston in search of the quality hides, tallow, and other cattle by products.[4]

The Hispanic missions actually began exporting hides and tallow after a deal was struck between a British com-pany and Father President Mariano Payeras of La Purísima Concepción Mission in 1822. Demand in New England and England for these products became so intense that by the 1830s they became California's principal exports. It is estimated that Boston traders alone may have bought some six million hides and seven thousand tons of tallow from 1826 to 1848. (Fontana, 217; Rosaldo, 9) Thus, Yankee traders early on had become so impressed with the natural resources of California and with the riches to be made from ranching and agriculture that even before the gold rush there was much interest in extending United States dominion to the West Coast.

Under the Mexican Republic, founded in 1821, many more land grants were issued for California lands than under Spanish rule. This placing of lands in the hands of civilians was a concerted policy of the liberal government of the new republic, which was curbing the power of the church by secularizing the missions and breaking up their large land holdings. Many of these grants became the basis of an ever-expanding ranching industry. More than four hundred land grants were issued between 1833 and 1846 for tracts of land ranging from four thousand to one hundred thousand acres. By the time of the U.S. takeover, there were more than eight million acres held by some eight hundred ranchers. Under the United States, the ranching way of life soon succumbed

Lugo Family of California.
Courtesy Los Angeles County Museum of Natural History.

to most changes. Most of the large tracts of land fell into the hands of speculators, land plungers, and railroad rights-of-way, paving the way for the concentration of large land holdings in the hands of few owners who would become the builders of California's giant agribusiness. By 1889, one-sixth of the farms in the state produced more than two-thirds of the crops. (Rosaldo, 159)

By the 1830s, cattle ranching spread from California westward to Hawaii and northward to northern Oregon. In 1832, King Kamehameha III of Hawaii arranged for Mexican va*queros* to come to Hawaii from California to teach ranching skills to the Hawaiians, giving birth to the cattle industry in the Hawaiian Islands. Cattle had actually been introduced by George Vancouver in 1793, and horses—California mustangs—by Richard J. Cleveland in 1803, but the cattle had been allowed to run wild and only in the 1820s had they begun to be hunted for their hides, tallow, and meat. The Hawaiian word for cowboy, *pianolo,* derives from the word *español* (Spaniard), and many of the techniques and traditions of the Hawaiian industry are owed to the Hispanic cowboy.

In 1837, Philip Edwards drove cattle from California north to Oregon, thus opening up the Northwest for ranching, with the help of California *vaqueros.* And ranchers in Oregon established the tradition of employing Mexican-American cowboys in the late nineteenth and early twentieth centuries; they came to comprise up to half of the cowhands. In 1869, again, six Mexican-American cowboys led by Juan Redón drove three thousand head of cattle for John Devine, who established the largest ranch in Oregon. Redón stayed on to work as Devine's foreman. (Slatta, 167)

Spain also had one of the oldest sheep cultures in the Old World, and it introduced the *churro,* a small, lean animal that gave coarse wool and could endure long marches and all types of weather. The *churro* became so acclimated to New Mexico and the Southwest that it became the basis for the large sheep industry that would develop over the centuries. In about 1876, fine merino sheep were brought by Anglos from the eastern seaboard and crossed with the *churros* to produce hybrid animals that gave a better quality wool and were ideally acclimated to the environment. By 1880, the Southwest was producing four million pounds of wool per year. (Slatta, 20–22)

In New Mexico, as elsewhere in the Southwest and the rest of Spanish America, it was the Hispanicized Indians who became the cowboys and shepherds over the centuries, especially because much of ranching originated in and around the missions. The Spaniards also taught the Indians to weave wool, and they became the power, especially Navajo women in the early nineteenth century, in the textile industry in New Mexico.

The large land grants that Spain and Mexico had given to individuals, along with grazing rights, not only facilitated the development of large cattle and sheep ranching for Hispanics, but this particular inheritance was passed on to Anglos when they came into the Southwest: a Mexican homestead in the Southwest consisted of 4,470 acres, twenty-eight times the size of an Anglo-American homestead in the Ohio Valley. The Spanish and Mexican land-use system was much better adapted to an arid environment, and facilitated the growth of the cattle industry on the open range within that environment. (Rosaldo, 5–8, 13)

Another industry that was somewhat related to the care and use of livestock was freighting, and Hispanics in the Southwest were the pioneers and masters of this industry. By the time of the arrival of the Anglos, there were well-established companies, routes, and technologies. Even with the arrival of Anglos, Mexican freighters continued to prosper. In 1856, Joaquín Quiroga laid the foundations for the lucrative freighting business in Arizona by carrying the first load of goods from Yuma to Tucson in his fourteen-mule pack train. In the next decades of Anglo domination, Mexican entrepreneurs continued as the major owners of freighting companies, linking the California coast with the Arizona and New Mexico territories, Baja California, and northern Mexico. They even reached as far east as Missouri.

One of the most important companies, Ochoa & Tully actually became the largest Hispanic company in Arizona in 1875. Estevan Ochoa's company was second only in the overall community to E. N. Fish & Company, handling some $300,000 in transactions per year. By 1880, his Tully, Ochoa & Company was the largest taxpayer in Pima County. Expanding from the long-distance hauling of freight by mule train, Ochoa and his partner, Pickney Randolph Tully, went into the mercantile business with stores that depended on their freight hauling. Thus they were among the first businessmen on the frontier to implement vertical integration. They also invested in mining and raising sheep. At the beginning of the 1880s, they were grazing fifteen thousand sheep and operating a wool processing factory, in addition to a settlement started at a camp where they raised sheep, which eventually became the town of Ochoaville. Ochoa is credited with having introduced to Tucson and surroundings a number of industrial technologies for turning out woolen blankets that had been developed in factories back East. (Sheridan, 42–40)

The importance of the freight hauling business by mule and wagon train subsided only with the introduction of the railroads, and then some of these same entrepreneurs made the transition to hauling freight and people by wagon and stagecoach to secondary and outlying communities. While Hispanics had followed trails blazed and used by Indians for centuries, the Hispanics pioneered most of the techniques and opened most of the trails that would later be used for trade and communications during the territorial and early statehood periods. In fact, some of today's major highways run along those routes pioneered for trade by Hispanics and Mexicans. (Sheridan, 43–45)

Somewhat related to freighting and the dependence on horse and carriage for transportation and commerce was the carriage industry, long practiced and supported by Hispanics. Of the many Hispanic blacksmiths and carriage makers that provided services in the Southwest, one stands out: Mexican immigrant Federico Ronstadt, who in 1889 founded a carriage business that became the largest carriage builder in Tucson, Arizona, and the region, including Sonora, Mexico. At its height, Ronstadt's wagon shop and hardware store employed sixty-five people who, besides repairing vehicles of all kinds, manufactured wagons, buggies, harnesses, and saddles. Ronstadt executed most of the iron forging himself and became known as one of the finest wagon and carriage makers in the Southwest. His business territory extended from California to Sonora, Mexico, where he had agents in Cananea, Nogales, Hermosillo, and Guaymas. By 1910, approximately one-third of Ronstadt's business was conducted south of the border. Ronstadt also marketed nationally known brands of wagons and farm machinery. (Sheridan, 94–95)

Horses were introduced into areas that became the United States by the Spaniards, beginning in Florida as early as 1521. Antonio de Mendoza was the first to bring horses to the mainland of the Americas specifically for breeding purposes in 1535, in Mexico. By 1650, there were countless herds of mustangs in northwest Mexico; they later made their way into the Great Plains of North America. The first breeding herds of horses were brought to Florida by Pedro Menéndez de Avilés in 1565. Juan de Oñate's colonization of New Mexico brought more horses north in 1598. During the next three centuries, Santa Fe, New Mexico, served as the center for distribution of horses, many of which became trading staples along the Santa Fe Trail to Kansas City, Missouri (an old Spanish trading post), and the United States. (Bennett and Hoffman, 107–108)

In 1539, Hernando de Soto brought a herd of pigs from Florida to Arkansas, and numerous pigs escaped along his path. These became the foundation for the feral populations of North America. Later, populations of domestic and feral pigs were introduced by the Franciscan missionaries to Texas and elsewhere. The razorback prized by hunters throughout the South arose from these populations. (Bennett and Hoffmann, 103)

Landing of de Soto. Courtesy Library of Congress.

Textiles and Handicrafts

Also related to the livestock industry and to agriculture in general were the textile industry and handicrafts. The Spaniards and mestizos depended on Indian labor to cultivate and care for many of the products from ranching and farming. Colonial industry in the Spanish colonies was built on the craftsmanship of the Indians who wove cotton and wool and used beautiful, durable dyes. The wood, stone, and metal work of the Indians was also prized, but the textile industry was one of the most widespread and successful industries, with cotton and wool mills multiplying in Mexico and Peru. By 1800, the textile industry became third in importance after agriculture and mining.

New Agricultural Products

In addition to the agriculture introduced by the Spaniards, the Native Americans contributed the results of thousands of years of crop cultivation that the Spaniards in turn introduced to Europe and that would come to feed the rest of the world for centuries. Most important of these were corn and potatoes, two staples that have been adopted almost worldwide. Included among the other products were numerous varieties of tubers and yams, tomatoes, manioc, new species of nuts and melons, vanilla cacao (chocolate), quinine, coca, ipecac, sarsaparilla, and tobacco. The Mexican Indians also introduced the Spaniards to the turkey—long before the pilgrims' Thanksgiving in Massachusetts. All the technologies and traditions of these agricultural products were later taught and transferred to Anglo-Americans in the South and Southwest of what would become the United States, if they had not already entered Anglo culture through Spanish introduction to Europe.

Mining

Of course, one of the most important industries was mining, and Spain in the colonial period did all that it could to further the technologies involved. By 1790, schools of mining were founded in Mexico City and Guatemala City. Much of the movement to settle and develop the north of New Spain was for the development of silver mining. In fact, the social and cultural transformation of the Central Corridor of New Spain up into what is today Arizona emerged during the colonial period as an extension and reflection of mining society. Mining culture and technology depended on the use of large numbers of human and material resources. A pattern developed wherein the missionaries acculturated the Indians, who were first used as forced labor in the mines. But within a few years, they became wage laborers in the mines and on the large haciendas that produced cattle and sheep to feed the mining population and supply leather. Soon, hundreds of thousands of mestizos, poor whites, and

New Almadén Mine. Courtesy Library of Congress.

acculturated Indians poured into the Central Corridor to work in the mines and haciendas. They began to form the backbone of a vast proletariat that supported two corollary industries, mining and ranching, and the development of a culture that would characterize the Southwest of the United States.

The silver mining technology that was developed by Hispanics involved the patio amalgamation process to free the silver from its ore base. The ore was excavated from a large shaft and then sifted, pulverized by a huge oxen-drawn wheel, gauged, and spread out into large pancakes. Mercury was then applied to free the sliver from the pancake. "Each step required thousands of workers, technicians, machines and beasts of burden and vast amounts of resources, such as rope, leather and iron." (Rosales, 1990, 12–13)

Hispanic expertise in mining resulted in important technological advances, especially in California. Sutters Mill was not the first non-Indian gold "discovery" in California. The first man to discover and mine gold in California was a Mexican herdsman by the name of Francisco López. He made his find on March 19, 1842, in Feliciano Canyon near Los Angeles. Mexicans worked diggings from Los Angeles up to Santa Cruz from this time on, years prior to James Marshall's discovery at Sutters Mill on January 24, 1848, which led to the California gold rush. (Meier and Rivera, 200–201)

Almost as important as the discovery of gold was an essential element for the mining process: mercury. And mercury was found in California very close to where it was needed by the gold rushers. In 1845, Andrés Castillero, a Mexican army captain, discovered mercury in red cinnabar rocks close to San José, California, and founded the very important New Almadén Mine and mining town with local Indian and Mexican workers. But the outbreak of the Mexican War and his need for finances ended his and his workers' business. By

1850, the British company of Barron and Forbes had bought the mine, and it was later taken over by the New York Quicksilver Mining Corporation. The mine became the second largest producer of quicksilver in the world during the remainder of the nineteenth century. (Meier and Feliciano, 253–255)

A SYSTEM OF JUSTICE

In 1511, the Spanish system of justice was instituted in the New World with the introduction of the *audiencia,* which, besides serving as a court, took on administrative and political functions. The first *audiencia* was founded in Santo Domingo and the second in New Spain in 1525. In 1524, King Charles V established the Council of the Indies, designed to oversee the administration of the colonies in the New World. The council effectively transplanted Spanish government and social organization to the Americas, administering courts of justice, authorizing land grants, counseling, and reporting to the king. Many of the laws and systems of government instituted under Spanish, and later Mexican, rule in the Southwest have been recognized and/or incorporated into the legal codes of the southwestern United States. Especially relevant are laws pertaining to ranching, farming, mining, jurisdictions, irrigation, and water rights. Furthermore, in 1512, in order to curb the abuse of the Indians by Spaniards, the Spanish crown established the first European colonial code, the Laws of Burgos, based on three principals, which although not followed and policed effectively, were revolutionary in the advance of human rights: (1) The Indians were free men, not slaves, (2) they were to be converted to Christianity by peaceful means, not by force, and (3) they were to be made to work. From this point on, the enslavement of the Indians was forbidden by law. Unfortunately, this law did not extend to African slaves. Slavery was

37

abolished in most Spanish-American countries in the early nineteenth century when they gained their independence from Spain.

The sheer amount of legal and civil work accomplished by the Spaniards was so voluminous that in 1681 Spain had to issue an abbreviated compilation of the Laws of the Indies, *Recopilación de las leyes de las Indias*, reducing the total to some fifty-four hundred laws applicable to the American colonies. By 1635, there had been issued some four hundred thousand edicts!

With the founding of Santa Fe, New Mexico, in 1610, many Spanish laws governing all facets of life were introduced to what would become the culture of the Southwest. Foremost among those laws were those concerning water and its management, many of which would pass into the legal codes of the United States. In the Spanish and Mexican judicial systems, the rights of the community weighed more heavily than those of the individual as concerned the precious resource of water in the arid Southwest. The water in Spanish and Mexican towns and cities was held in trust for the benefit of the entire community. The *cabildo,* the democratically elected town council, held authority over local water usage. Usually, each pueblo was invested with special water

Cabildo—*seat of city government built by the Spanish in New Orleans.*
Courtesy Library of Congress.

rights. Title to the water in streams flowing through the pueblo's common lands was reserved to the pueblo and its inhabitants for both domestic and public use, as in parks and nonagricultural purposes. The Treaty of Guadalupe Hidalgo ending the Mexican War passed these rights on to posterity. The city of Los Angeles, for example, which inherited the pueblo rights, was able to obtain a favorable ruling from the U.S. Supreme Court over a water dispute with landowners of the San Fernando Valley. The Court ruled that the city had prior claim to all waters originating within the watershed of the Los Angeles River, thus asserting that "pueblo rights" took precedence over the common law rights of the landowners. (Meyer, 156–157; Rosaldo, 13)

In 1767, Spanish laws governing water usage also became the foundation for what would become today's Texas laws regarding water usage and rights. It is estimated that Spain and Mexico granted some 26 million of Texas's 170 million acres to colonizers, and various types of water rights were attached to these land grants. The water rights that went with these grants are still covered by Texas law but determined by the terms of the original grants. After the founding of the Texas Republic in 1836 and then the later admission of Texas as a state to the Union, the Spanish and Mexican laws regarding water usage were incorporated into the state constitution. This Spanish heritage was the basis of the Irrigation Act of 1852, which is the basis for Texas statutory irrigation law. (Dobkins, ix–x, 124–125)

At the time of establishing its republic and later when becoming a state of the union, Texas in particular held on to many laws from Hispanic tradition, especially those regarding family law, land, and property. In 1839, Texas adopted the first Homestead Law in an area that would become part of the United States. Homestead Law is based on the principle of protecting certain pieces of personal property from creditors and has its roots in Castilian practices that date to the thirteenth century and were passed into Texas state law from the Hispano-Mexican legal codes. This practice made it possible for a debtor to protect the principal residence of the family from seizure by creditors; it also protected other basic items, such as clothing and implements of trade, needed for the debtor to make a living. Today, Texas continues to have one of the strongest property exemption laws of any state. Texas also accepted the Mexican and Spanish land use system via this law, which called for large tracts of land with access to water that could be used for ranching cattle and sheep. (Chipman, 253–254; McKnight, 9; Rosaldo, 13)

In 1840, the Texas legislature adopted the Hispano-Mexican system of a single court rather than continuing the dual court system (courts of law and courts of equity) of Anglo-American law. Under the Hispanic system, all issues could be considered simultaneously rather divided between two jurisdictions. Thus, the Republic of Texas became the first English-speaking country to adopt a permanent and full unitary system of justice. (Chipman, 250–251) Also in 1840, the Texas legislature adopted from the Hispanic legal system the principle that a person must be sued in the locale in which he resides, for his convenience. These two principles passed into Texas state law. (Chipman, 251)

That same legislative session of the Republic of Texas adopted and subsequently passed on to the state legal code the Spanish legal concept of community property. Husband and wife were to share equally in the profits and fruits of their marriage. Under Anglo-American law, however, property belonged exclusively to the husband, and on the death of her spouse, the wife was protected only by a life-interest in one-third of the lands of her deceased spouse. The Republic of Texas recognized this inequity and specifically excluded the Anglo-American law that limited a wife's interests. The previously Hispanic provinces of Texas and Louisiana were the first to protect wives through common-law statutes. Today, community property law is prevalent in states that have an Hispanic heritage: Texas, Louisiana, New Mexico, Arizona, Nevada, and California. It has also been pointed out that even the right to file a joint income tax return derives from the Spanish principle. (Chipman, 253; McKnight, 8; Rosaldo, 13–14)

That all-important Texas legislative session of 1840 incorporated into the legal code of Texas the Spanish concept of "independent executor" in relation to probate matters (i.e., wills). This did away with the Anglo-American legal practice of executors obtaining court orders to perform acts not specifically called for in the testament. Placing confidence in an executor was more expedient and saved legal expenses both for the legal system and the individuals involved. This Spanish judicial procedure later spread from Texas to Arizona, Washington, Idaho, and some ten other states as provisions of the Uniform Probate Code. (Chipman, 251)

Numerous other principles of Spanish family law were incorporated into the legal code of Texas in 1841; they covered the rights of partners in marriage as well as the adoption of children. Included among these principles was the protection of the rights of parties in a common law relationship. Furthermore, children of such marriages, even if proven invalid later, were considered legitimate, and a fair division of the profits of marriage had to result. This legitimation of children is still part of Texas family law today. (Chipman, 252)

In 1850, Texas reinstated into its legal code the Spanish principle of adopting children after it had been dropped ten years earlier under the new legal code of the Republic of Texas. The concept of adoption was not recognized in English law, and Anglo-American law continued this glaring gap. Because of numerous petitions for specific rulings on adoptions during the Republic and early statehood of Texas, the legislature decided to reinstate the Hispanic concept of adoption, including the right of adopted children to inherit their adopted parents' estates. In Texas, as in the Hispanic world, the rights of an adopted child became the same as those of biological children, and they can still claim inheritance from their bloodline parents too. With the exception of Mississippi, Texas was the first Anglo-American state to permanently recognize and codify adoption. (Chipman, 252–253; McKnight, 7)

To one degree or another, the other states of the Southwest reflect the base of Hispano-Mexican law. An important precedent of nondiscriminatory law was set in the adoption of the constitution for the state of California. In 1849, at the California constitutional convention, Anglos resisted giving the vote to Indians, Blacks, and mestizos. But largely through the leadership of Hispanic delegates, the convention came to an agreement that any person who had been considered a Mexican citizen, regardless of race, would be so considered under the constitution of California. This was the first time that a state constitution defined citizenship based on the inclusiveness of all races, as was the case in Mexico. However, those Blacks and Indians who had not been Mexicans would be excluded. (Gómez-Quiñones, 226–227)

The constitutions of California, Colorado, New Mexico, and Texas all recognized Spanish as an official language of the state and called for laws to be published in both English and Spanish. The New Mexico Constitution, adopted in 1619, specifically authorized use of the Spanish language in voting. Article VII of the New Mexico Constitution provides for the "right of any citizen to vote, hold office, or sit upon juries, shall never be restricted, abridged or impaired on account of religion, race, language or color, or inability to speak, read or write the English or Spanish languages … ." The constitution, under Article II, specifically incorporated the rights of the people of New Mexico under the Treaty of Guadalupe Hidalgo, which was a product of the war with Mexico. In addition, the state was officially bilingual, as provided for by its constitution: "All laws passed by the Legislature shall be published in both the English and Spanish languages," and the legislature was mandated to provide funds for the training of teachers to be proficient in both English and Spanish (Article XII). Article XII also prohibited segregation for the children of "Spanish descent." (Gómez-Quiñones, 325–328)

In these states where anti-immigrant and English-Only movements are so virulent today, very few agitators and nativists are mindful of the statutory basis for use of the Spanish language in public affairs.

THE ARTS

The arts, the music, and the visual imagery of Spain were immediately introduced to the Native Americans as part of the evangelizing effort, and of course portraits of saints and scenes from the Old and New Testaments adorned the interiors of churches that were constructed. Both the architecture and the decoration of the churches and other edifices soon evolved styles that were composites of European and Native American arts.

The Spaniards also supported the fine arts as separate from religion and evangelization. By 1700, operas were not only performed but composed in Mexico City and Lima. In fact, San Francisco's great operatic tradition began in 1847 when the Alvarez Grand Opera Company was lured by a $10,000 subscription from Lima to California for a season in the city by the bay. (McGroarty, 378) In 1750, the first symphony orchestra in the Americas was organized in Caracas, Venezuela.

One of the greatest colonial artists, José Campeche (1751–1809), was a mulatto born the son of a freed slave in San Juan, Puerto Rico. Campeche was the leading portrait artist of the nobility and the government in Puerto Rico, and his reputation grew, leading him to the most important commissions for religious painting in the nearby colonies and Puerto Rico. Throughout the Spanish colonies, there are similar examples of artists who were instructed in European styles, were offered significant apprenticeships with Spanish masters, and rose to prominence in their own and neighboring colonies and provinces.

In most of the Spanish colonies, sculpture was at first relegated to religious statuary, but in Puebla, Mexico, there developed an important school of sculpture that went beyond the religious, headed by Manuel Tolsá (1757–1816), who was also a noted architect. His most famous piece is the *Caballito,* an equestrian sculpture of Charles IV, which still stands in Mexico City. Tolsá is credited with introducing neoclassical art into Mexico. By 1783, academies of fine arts were founded in Mexico and Guatemala. It was these artistic traditions and references that the missionaries and colonizers brought with them on entering the lands north of the Rio Grande.

The history of theater in a European language in what became the continental United States begins with the soldiers who performed and improvised plays during Juan de Oñate's colonizing expedition to New Mexico in 1598; a

Captain Marcos Farfán de los Godos wrote plays based on the events of the journey. Among the colonizers and missionaries of both the Oñate expedition and the early expeditions to Florida were poets who wrote and later published extensive narrative epics about the expeditions and encounters with native populations: Gaspar Pérez de Villagrá's *La Conquista de la Nueva México* (The Conquest of New Mexico) and Alonso Gregorio de Escobedo's *La Florida*. Written literary tradition in a European language begins here in North America above the Rio Grande.

Frontispiece for Alvar Núñez Cabeza de Vaca's La relación. *Courtesy Arte Público Press.*

A RICH LEGACY, BUT A LEGACY DEMEANED

This very brief exposition of the Hispanic legacy, which is also part of the heritage of all of the peoples of the United States, indicates the level and extent of cultural riches that the United States inherited when it expanded its southern and western borders, and when it broadened its sphere of political and economic interests to include the Caribbean, Mexico, and Central America. The cultural baggage brought with each Hispanic encompassed within the new borders or with each Hispanic immigrant, is the product of centuries of development and, even before the United States was founded, had predetermined many fundamental aspects—be they economic, artistic, or spiritual—of life as we know it today in the American republic.

So why have Hispanics been cast in negative images throughout the history of the United States? Why has United States policy toward Spanish America been so authoritarian, domineering, and xenophobic? Why have Mexicans, in particular, been subjected to cycles of labor recruitment and then inhumane deportation by the United States in what cannot be seen as anything but a love-hate relationship? How do we as a nation rationalize our stereotype of the lazy Mexican asleep under a cactus while importing him to perform the most laborious jobs our economy has to offer? How do we fashion our identity as an enlightened democracy and at the same time create, promote, and support authoritarian regimes in Spanish America? How do we rationalize our swallowing up half of Mexican national territory as well as appropriating Puerto Rico and the Virgin Islands as colonies?

Chapter Two

THE
BLACK
LEGEND

As DISCUSSED, OUR MINDSET AS A SOCIETY toward Hispanic peoples began to be fashioned long before Anglos encountered Spanish Americans. The seeds of Hispanophobia took root in the European nations that were vigorously attempting to check the growth of the Spanish Empire during its ascendancy in the Renaissance: Italians, Germans, French, English, and Dutch all took part. Hispanophobia later intensified when the English, French, and Dutch challenged Spain's hegemony in the New World and competed with the Catholic monarchs and their royal descendants to establish colonies in the Americas. From the fifteenth century on, the Spanish soldiers and lords who had conquered and ruled vast portions of Italy and the Lowlands were depicted in oral and written lore as cruel, tyrannical, foppish, lazy, fanatical, and greedy, among other stereotypical characteristics.

The negative image of Spaniards was disseminated precisely during the time that the use of the printing press spread, before it did anyplace else, throughout northern Europe in the hands of some of Spain's greatest adversaries. The institution of the Inquisition in Spain in 1480 plus that country's expulsion of the Jews in 1492 and subsequent relocation to the Low Countries and Germany also had the effect of intensifying the barrage of anti-Spanish sentiment, as this more literate class of displaced Spaniards took to pen and press with a vengeance. Amsterdam and Frankfurt am Main became centers of publication that would issue anti-Spanish propaganda to further the battles of the European powers against the Spanish Empire.

More important was the Protestant Reformation in spreading the attacks against Spain as the leading defender of Catholicism. The charge of Spanish fanaticism and obscurantism became reinforced in the minds of Protestants throughout Europe and in the English colonies in North America. The process by which many of these anti-Spanish sentiments were developed and disseminated also marked the advent of a new tool in international relations: propaganda, a tool whose growth followed the rise of printing in Western society. The propaganda campaign also coincided with the rise of European capitalism and the economic value of New World colonies for England, Holland, and France. Added to this were the generations, if not centuries, of French and German perspectives on Spaniards as racially inferior, a people who were the product of miscegenation with Jews and Moslems.[5]

Spanish and Spanish-American scholars have come to know this propaganda campaign and the prejudices that it created as the "Black Legend." Its bigotry applies not only to Spain, but to Spanish Americans and all Hispanics, not only to the conquistadores but to their mixed-blood descendants—for miscegenation has also been anathema to Anglo and northern European peoples. In fact, it was Spain's hegemony in the New World that really fired the flames of the legend in order to justify, among other motives, the establishment of English, French, and Dutch colonies in the Americas. Yet Catholic popes had reserved the right to colonize solely for the Spanish and Portuguese; Spain and Portugal had priority in claim and colonization. The popular literature and official policies of the other colonial powers were based on the idea that Spaniards were uniquely cruel, greedy, and depraved in their conquest and fanatical conversion of the natives of the New World and in their colonization of their lands. Of course, this is a fallacy not born out by historical investigation; scholars have gone to lengths to favorably compare Spanish policies toward the Indians with those of the English (and even the Germans in Venezuela), the extent to which the Indians were governed and/or protected by the Spanish, their relative acquisitiveness and hunger for precious metals, etc. (Powell, 14–29) The fact that Spain governed such expansive and diverse regions of the Americas for nearly three centuries in numerical inferiority to the masses of Indians and then gave rise to a biologically and culturally mixed civilization speaks eloquently to the colonizing and evangelizing motives of the Spaniards and their methods of implementation. Today, Spanish is the language most spoken in the hemisphere and Catholicism is the predominant religion. This was not the feat of a people who solely came to plunder mineral wealth and then return to the home country or to reap the riches of the New World while exterminating or pushing aside the original inhabitants.

The initial phase of Spanish contact with the Indians was the bloodiest and most brutal—and it was the phase most graphically written about by polemicists. However, as Spanish policy evolved, conquest and colonization became more peaceful, efficient, and humane, with numerous new laws and policies implemented, as stated earlier, to protect the Indians and facilitate their assimilation into Spanish civilization. In extending their institutions to the New World, the Spaniards had to innovate when it came to the Indians. They had never

49

Conquest scene. Courtesy Library of Congress.

encountered similar peoples before; their only remotely similar experience had been in their crusade against the Moslems
who had occupied the Iberian Peninsula for seven hundred
years. Their specific papal charge was to bring the Natives
into the light of Christianity, and their three centuries of relations were characterized by progressively more humane laws
and measures to ensure the Indians' civil rights, education,
and faith.

> Spain's three centuries of tutelage and official concern for
> the welfare of the American Indian is a record not equaled
> by other Europeans in overseas government of peoples of
> lesser, or what were considered lesser, cultures. For all the
> mistakes, for all the failures, for all the crimes committed,
> and even allowing the Crown motives of practicality and
> self-service, in its overall performance Spain, in relation to
> the American Indian, need offer no apology to any other
> people or nation. (Powell, 25)

It is precisely that Spain was grappling to understand the
cultures of the New World, the potential interrelationships

of Spaniards and Natives, and it is precisely Spain's recognition of atrocities and abuses committed by its people
that led to an open debate not only tolerated but furthered
by the Crown.

   The first real debater and the one most responsible for
fueling the anti-Spain propaganda machine was Friar
Bartolomé de las Casas, a Dominican who eventually was able
to reform Spain's policies toward the Indians. He had a great
deal of influence on the passage in 1542 of the New Laws of
the Indies, which reaffirmed the illegality of enslavement of
the Indians. Throughout his crusade, Las Casas rose to
prominence, was officially promoted to the rank of bishop,
and named the Protector of the Indians by the Crown. From

Bartolomé de las Casas. Courtesy Library of Congress.

the early 1550s, Las Casas published his arguments on behalf of the Indians' humanity and civil rights, supporting his arguments with exaggerated and distorted examples of abuse, torture, dismemberment, and destruction of the Indians by the Spaniards in the Indies. Las Casas was one of the creators of the myth of the "noble savage," whom he contrasted with the Spanish "wolves and tigers."

Today, there is no apologizing that can be done for the *encomienda,* a system that was instituted during early colonization to reap the benefit of the Indians' labor, which they exchanged only for the benefits of conversion to Christianity. As quasi-slavery, the Indians' role was bitterly attacked by Las Casas and others. But the fervor and zeal of his arguments turned to excessive distortion in his *Brevísima relación de la destrucción de las Indias* (Brief Account of the Destruction of the Indies), in which he claimed that the Spaniards had killed some twenty million Indians during the conquest, a figure that was purely his own invention, an horrific feat that would have been impossible for the number of Spaniards in the Indies to accomplish, a figure that even the indigenous agriculture of the time could not have sustained in the populations of the islands named by Las Casas.

The *Brief Account,* an accomplished piece of propaganda on behalf of a worthy cause, became the most translated and illustrated chronicle of the conquest and colonization in Europe. It was first issued in French in 1578, then in Dutch in 1579 and English in 1583. With all of its obvious distortions, untruths, and excesses, it was read as history, and it became the centerpiece of the propaganda attack that would serve well the interests of the other European colonial powers, particularly England. Las Casas's tract was disseminated in Europe at precisely the time that England was in ascendancy and challenging Spain's monopoly on the New World.

Las Casas's depiction of the greedy and inhumane Spaniards rendered them unfit in European eyes to govern the New World, and both political and violent battle against the Spaniards would be justified and worthy.

Already in the 1560s the Low Countries were rebelling against Spanish governance and had initiated a propaganda campaign through printing presses that came to be known as The Paper War.[6] When England's schismatic separation from the Catholic Church was confirmed in 1558 with the ascension of Elizabeth to the throne, the Dutch and the English together attacked the Spanish "papists" who were leading the Counter Reformation. But it was the Dutch pursuit for independence from Spain that really relied on the publication of pamphlets to inflame the citizenry against its King, Philip II, Spain, and Rome as well. In these pamphlets Las Casas's exaggerations had particular poignancy, and the example of the abuse of the Indians was hammered home over and over again, as can be seen in this preface to a 1603 Dutch edition of the *Brief Account:*

> The Spanish monster slyly attacks you. As they murdered the Indian lords, they have also killed many of your princes, so as to further tyrannize over you; which they did not spare, which they showed in Zuthpen, Naarden, and also Harlem. As long as you keep the Spaniard in the nest; as long as he builds fortresses in your towns that, like a pest, infect the whole country; as long as you quench the bloodthirsty Spanish desire. So long you remain like the Indians, unfree. So, drive away the Spanish tyranny![7]

The anti-Spanish message was repeated so often and so intensely that to this day many of the stereotypes created in this propaganda still prevail in northern Europe. The outcome has been summarized by Powell as follows:

53

> Anti-Spanish, anti-Catholic propaganda became in Dutch
> hands widely and deeply imbedded in the general
> Protestant tradition, the result of effective linking of the
> Dutch Revolt with French, English, and German inter-
> ests. And that part of the Netherlands that eventually
> achieved independence, uncritically absorbed as an
> integral part of its nationality the deep hispanophobia,
> with all its distortions, that was so successfully propa-
> gated in the early years. This propaganda, in short,
> became Dutch popular history. (Powell, 64)

In the late sixteenth and early seventeenth centuries,
England's nationalism developed as the country began to create an overseas empire and fully institute its Protestantism
from the top down to the populace. In its growing national
identity, England saw Spain as its natural enemy, both because
of Spain's monopoly of the New World and its championship
of Catholicism. It was to England's benefit to support the Dutch
rebellion against Spain, first because of England's own imperialistic intentions, and second because of its battle against the
papacy. The culmination of various political events furthered
the anti-Spanish cause in England: (1) Spain's hegemony in
Europe began to decline in the 1640s with its loss in the Thirty
Years' War and the confirmation of Dutch independence, and
(2) in 1688, a descendant of William of Orange assumed the
English throne, confirming the Dutch-English alliance and
marking a victory for the Protestants over the Catholics in
England. Throughout, the propaganda stream was unabated,
marked by continuous influence and support from printers
in Holland and Germany. But the English version of the Black
Legend developed some unique features:

> For one thing, the English have shown little interest in
> criticizing Spanish intellectual standards. Instead, they
> have created a formidable stereotype of the Spaniard
> himself which comprises most of the vices and

shortcomings known to man. Readers of Anglo-Saxon historical novels are all too familiar with the general outline. When the Spaniard has the upper hand, his cruelty and hauteur are insupportable. When reduced to his proper stature by some unimpeachably Nordic hero, he is cringing and mean-spirited: a coward whose love of plots and treacheries is exceeded only by his incompetence in carrying them out. (Maltby, 6)

And much of English propaganda itself, such as the writings of Richard Hakluyt, was aimed at promoting English competition with Spain in the New World. Hakluyt's 1584 Discourse on the Western Planting advocated the colonization of Virginia while haranguing against Spanish cruelties and tyranny in the West Indies. Hakluyt and English pamphleteers were successful in furthering a passionate Hispanophobia. But it was one of Hakluyt's Flemish associates, an engraver and printer located in Frankfurt named Theodore De Bry, who

Theodore De Bry engraving of the torture of Indians by Spaniards. Courtesy Library of Congress.

was able to inflame Hispanophobia in Europe beyond the printed narrative to the graphically visual with his detailed illustrations of the atrocities narrated by Las Casas. From 1598 on, most editions of Las Casas's *Brief Account* included De Bry's engravings, which were even printed and distributed separately from Las Casas's text.

Some of the English pamphleteers indicted the mixed racial heritage of the Spaniards, decrying not only their Moslem and Jewish interbreeding but also their Visigothic roots:

> What humanitie, what faith, what courtesie, what modestie, and civilitie, may wee thinke to finde amongst the scumme of Barbarians? [Spain] is and ever hathe bene the sinke, the puddle, and filthie heape of the most lothsome, infected, and slavish people that ever yet lived on earth. ... This wicked race of those half Wisigots ... . This demie Moore, demie Jew, yea demie Saracine. ... What? Shall those Marranos, yes, those impious Atheists reigne over us kings and Princes? [Those Spaniards with] ... theyre insatiate avarice, theyre more than Tigrish cruelty, theyre filthy, monstruous and abominable luxurie ... theyre lustfull and inhumaine deflouring of their matrones, wives, daughters, theyre matchless and sodomiticall ravishings of young boyes, which these demi-brabarian Spaniardes committed. ... (cited in Powell, 76)

Numerous other pamphleteers railed against the "anti-Christian" Spanish, ironically wedding their battle against the papacy and Spain and making it a religious mission. One of the most famous, effective, and prolific pamphleteers of them all was the preacher Thomas Scott, who in the 1620s had many of his pamphlets printed in Holland and based many of his arguments on Las Casas's accusations. Scott persistently harangued against the "anti-Christian" Spaniards, helping incite England to war against Spain.

While printed pamphlets were fanatical and extremely imaginative in their Hispanophobic vitriol, another medium provided more direct access to the illiterate masses: theater. Throughout the Elizabethan period, English theater created and popularized anti-Spanish images, furthering some of the stereotypes that would persist for centuries. The Diego characters in Thomas Heywood's plays, for example, are notably "tyrannous, cruel, lascivious and bloody." (Cawley, 140) Caricatures and stereotypes of Spaniards were common in other leading Elizabethan playwrights, such as Middleton, Jonson, Peele, and Fletcher. But most serious of all was English playwrights' insistence on depicting the cruelty and injustice of the Spanish conquest and colonization of the Americas. As Powell points out, the English used Las Casas's depictions of Spanish actions in the Americas to "justify their capture of Spanish treasure and to portray their own virtues by contrast with Spanish villainy. ... The theme was extended to form part of a larger picture of English moral, racial, and religious superiority over the Spaniard." (Powell, 77–78) Through the stage, the pen, and the printing press,

> Elizabethan Englishmen parlayed defeat of the [Spanish] Armada, Bartolomé de las Casas, and a large envy into a vast, hypocritical, and unqualified superiority complex over the baser, less efficient, and more cowardly Spaniard. This was certainly a stimulus for empire building and not entirely unlike Spanish attitudes in defeating Moslems, discovering, exploring, colonizing and Christianizing a New World, with the helpful conviction that they were chosen by God for such important tasks. But the new, quickly solidified tradition of hate toward the inferior Spaniard distorted history and confused historians; grossly unfair to Spain and Spaniards since the British "tree of hate" bore so much evil fruit in the Western world; and very deceptive to many generations

of English-speaking schoolchildren whose education has
inherited the nearly unbridgeable gap of misunderstanding between Anglo and Hispanic cultures and people.
(Powell, 79)

England and Spain continued to be rivals, if not enemies,
into the nineteenth century. The Enlightenment in Europe
conveniently chose Spain and its Catholicism as targets for
derision and symbols of obscurantism. Of course these attitudes were passed on to England's colonies in North
America, and despite Spain's assistance to the thirteen colonies in their War of Independence, the intellectuals in the
newly founded United States not only harbored the
Hispanophobic attitudes of their ancestors, but they proceeded to treat Spain and its New World colonies as, if not
enemies, rivals—rivals for hegemony in the Western Hemisphere. Already in 1648 with the publication of Thomas
Gage's *The English-American,* the idea was becoming widely
disseminated that the iniquitous Spanish rule in the New
World could easily—militarily—be replaced by that of the
virtuous English Protestants. As Powell goes at length to
emphasize, "Our ancestors established themselves in
America during the seventeenth century, and this colonization process was nourished by their hatred of Spain and
their desire to break the Spanish New World monopoly."
(102) And, with the rise of the American Republic, the Spanish Black Legend provided the ugly image of the Hispanic
enemy that would fuel hateful speeches in Congress, yellow
journalism, and popular culture to justify the expansion of
the United States westward and southward.

In the intellectual modes that crystallized in the United
States during the nineteenth century—many of which have
extended to the present—there are several main lines where
popularization of Hispanophobic biases is clearly seen. Some

of the frontier clashes were still, irritatingly, with the Spanish (or Mexicans). In the Texan-Mexican struggle and then in the war with Mexico, some ingrained antipathy was transferred toward Catholic Spain to its American heirs. And Spain continued ruling and fighting rebellions in nearby Cuba, leading to disagreeable incidents that kept alive the ancient antagonisms. This abrasive proximity to persons of Spanish speech, especially a darker-hued Mexican (remember those long-ago German disparagements of the smaller, darker men of Iberia?), encouraged our faith in Nordic superiority. It was a small step, really, from "Remember the Armada" to "Remember the Alamo." Highly intemperate utterances in the United States Congress and elsewhere contained abusive references to Latin America's Spanish past and advocated U.S. takeover of those lands, at least as far as Panama, and sometimes beyond. And, as we shall see, at the century's end a heady mixture of Darwinism, war with Spain, and faith in a kind of Nordic manifest destiny heightened superior race concepts in the Anglo-American mind. (Powell, 118)

The early Americans soon found an ideology that would allow them to replace the "iniquitous Spanish" and their bastard progeny, at least in North America: Manifest Destiny.

Chapter Three

MANIFEST DESTINY ❖ ❖ ❖

THE RACIAL THOUGHT OF WESTERN EUROPE found fertile ground in the nascent United States, a uniquely successful republican enterprise, so that it could bear its logical fruit: a widespread belief that Anglo-Saxon Americans were a separate, uniquely superior people destined to bring good government and Christianity to vast regions of the world, to govern over the racially inferior inhabitants, or to drive them into extinction in order to develop the natural resources God had willed to the Anglo-Saxon race. American racial thought was most directly inherited from the English, who themselves had inherited a long Teutonic tradition relating to the origins of nomadic Germanic tribes that practiced a rudimentary democracy and political liberty. The English and then later the Americans believed that they were enjoying a freedom and form of government practiced earlier by Anglo-Saxons far back in the Middle Ages, and that the Anglo-Saxons in the New World had been chosen by God to inherit and further these freedoms and political organization, while reaping the wealth and power that was also their God-given destiny. Underpinning this messianic ideology was the Romantic belief, which had grown up over centuries, that the

Anglo-Saxons had developed out of a purely Aryan racial strain that had been responsible for civilizing much of Europe and now would spread civilization across the North American continent and even make the great leap across the Pacific to Asia. The imprecise and fanciful definitions and usage of the term "Anglo-Saxon" originally, and erroneously, referred to some fifth-century Germanic tribes that had settled in England. By the time the term reached the western regions of North America, it came to describe the white people of North America, a sort of American race, in opposition to Indians, Mexicans, Spaniards, and Chinese.[8]

> By 1850 a clear pattern was emerging. From their own successful past as Puritan colonists, Revolutionary patriots, conquerors of a wilderness, and creators of an immense material prosperity, the Americans had evidence plain before them that they were the chosen people; from the English they had learned that the Anglo-Saxons had always been particularly gifted in the arts of government; from the scientists and ethnologists they were learning that they were of a distinct Caucasian race, innately endowed with abilities that placed them above other races; from the philologists, often through literary sources, they were learning that they were descendants of those Aryans who followed the sun to carry civilization to the whole world. (Horsman, 5)

Just as furthering the Spanish Black Legend had much to do with the development of English nationalism and the English Reformation, so too was Henry VIII's break with Rome the motive for the development of a myth of an early Saxon church that practiced a purer Christianity. From 1530 to 1730, writers, preachers, and theorists claimed that this early church was just one of the superior institutions that could be traced back to the early Anglo-Saxons and ultimately to the courageous and high-principled Germanic tribes that Tacitus had described. These were the same ones who earlier on had destroyed the Roman Empire, and now their descendants would destroy the universal Roman Church.

As we have seen earlier, English nationalism was already highly racialized by the time of colonization. The English colonists in North America not only brought with them these racist myths and ideologies, but among them grew the idea that they would reform the English system of government by returning it to its earlier, purer form. And furthermore, as Horsman illustrates, "The colonists believed fully that the Anglo-Saxons were a particularly successful branch of the freedom-loving Germanic peoples described by Tacitus." (16) But it is in the writings of Thomas Jefferson that the theme of the freedom-loving Anglo-Saxons of early England is most present, and it was his emphasis on the Teutonic origins of Anglo-Saxons that was truly influential in transforming the emphasis on Anglo-Saxon society and institutions to an emphasis on a racial group. (Horsman, 19–20)

During the first half of the nineteenth century, Romantic writers in England and Germany idealized the Aryan race and its talents, with perhaps Walter Scott popularizing the Aryan vision the most in England and the United States. But there also developed during the same years the science of humans that began to insist on polygenesis for the races of the world and to couple with the physiological differences of these races their comparative achievements as societies and cultures. In this scheme, of course, the Anglo-Saxon/Teutonic/Caucasian race and culture were seen as far superior. Theorists did not have as much sway, however, as the Anglo-Saxons themselves confronting the other races in daily life in North America: black slaves and the "savage" Indians. Numerous reasons for alleged Native American and African inferiority developed among Americans, justifying

63

the institution of slavery and the continual expansion onto Indian lands—the justification later extended to Spanish and Mexican lands.

By the 1850s, American scientists had supplied ample "proof" that the Anglo-Saxon race was far superior to all others, and this particularly explained the success of the Anglo-Saxons in North America, their prosperity, and their ability to subordinate the other races. Practically from the outset, the Americans furthered the idea of populating the American continent with their own race, a homogeneous American people with "one language, one culture, and identical political institutions." (Horsman, 92) And quite often, from Jefferson to later thinkers, the continent—even South America—was thought of as being empty of other peoples (despite the full knowledge of the existence of Indians and Hispanics throughout the hemisphere). And, according to such widely read and influential writers as Josiah C. Nott and George R. Gliddon,[9] it was the destiny of the Anglo-Saxons to supplant the inferior races; in doing so, they were fulfilling a law of nature.

> Nations and races, like individuals, have each an especial destiny: some are born to rule, and others to be ruled … . No two distinctly-marked races can dwell together on equal terms. Some races, moreover, appear destined to live and prosper for a time, until the destroying race comes, which is to exterminate and supplant them. (Nott and Gliddon, 77)

The extinction, or even extermination of inferior races, was in the natural order as the superior races fulfilled their destiny. And clearly, if the Anglo-Saxons were to obey their God-ordained continental imperative, the Indians and the Mexicans were the inferior races that would have to cede the way or become extinct. The "scientific" writings of the period provided the rationales for such genocidic thought, with Nott leading the way with his beliefs about the Indian, whom he saw as "an untamable, carnivorous animal, which is fading away before civilization ... the race must soon be extinct—even the pure blood Mexicans, who I have no question are a different race from the aboriginal savage, are going down in darkness to their long home."[10] The Indian's "race is run, and probably he has performed his earthly mission. He is now gradually disappearing, to give place to a higher order of beings. The order of nature must have its course."[11] Scores of practitioners in the new "science of man" were popularizing racialist theories that justified the superior Anglo-Saxons' displacement of the lesser races in North America and heavily influencing government policy towards the Indians, Mexicans, and Hispanics in the Caribbean. As Horsman has stated:

> ... striking was the manner in which the new ideas became a topic of popular discussion. By 1850 the natural inequality of races was a scientific fact which was published widely. One did not have to read obscure books to know that Caucasians were innately superior, and that they were responsible for civilization in the world, or to know that inferior races were destined to be overwhelmed or even to disappear. These ideas permeated the main American periodicals and in the second half of the century formed part of the accepted truth of America's schoolbooks.[12] (Horsman, 157)

By the mid-nineteenth century, after successfully taking almost half of the national territory of Mexico as a spoil of war, supporters of racial expansionist destiny became even more aggressive, voicing their militancy in periodicals and pressing the government to expand, conquer, or otherwise incorporate the West, the Caribbean, and the remainder of Mexico: "Cuba will be Americanized—will own the sway of our race, as will St. Domingo, the West India Islands, generally, and all Mexico, in our time," stated an editorialist in *Southern Quarterly Review* in 1852.[13]

The fervor for conquest and expansion was furthered by a generation of Romantic creative writers who picked up the tradition of Anglo-Saxons' ordained superiority. One of the foremost of these was William Gilmore Simms. A southern writer who was nevertheless popular in the North, he promoted racial militancy in poems, essays, and novels. Simms championed the United States carrying its racialized civilization into Mexico by the sword during the Mexican War and afterward, always envisioning war as the greatest implement of civilized people: "War is the greatest element of modern civilization, and our destiny is conquest. Indeed the moment a nation ceases to extend its sway it falls prey to an inferior but more energetic neighbor."[14] In his championing of U.S. civilization's march to the Pacific and southward, he also celebrated the extension of slavery to those lands as "the greatest and most admirable agent of Civilization."[15] Simms also promoted the annexation of Cuba and even William Walker's seizing the presidency of Nicaragua, stating in 1857 that "filibustering is the moral necessity of all Anglo-Norman breed. It is the necessity of all progressive races."[16] While rejecting expansion through force, as in the Mexican War, Theodore Parker nevertheless believed the United States was destined to govern the entire hemisphere; the United States would be "the mother of a thousand Anglo-Saxon states, tropic and temperate on both sides of the equator .... The fulfillment of this vision is pure province; we are the involuntary instruments of God. Shall America scorn the mission God sends her on?"[17]

Even some of the greatest and most enduring writers and thinkers of the United States in the nineteenth century subscribed to many of these racialist ideas. While shunning the idea of racial purity, Ralph Waldo Emerson considered the English and their American offspring as having inherited a Norse primitive energy that drove them to advance civilization: "It is very certain that the strong British race, which have now overrun so much of this continent, most also overrun that tract [Texas], and Mexico and Oregon also, and it will in the course of ages be of small import by what particular occasions and methods it was done. It is a secular question."[18] Emerson saw in the English "the best stock in the world" and celebrated Anglo-Saxon drive, morality, and single-mindedness: "The Teutonic tribes have a national singleness of heart, which contrasts with the Latin races. The German name has a proverbial significance of sincerity and honest meaning."[19]

The racial imperative of the Anglo-Saxons to extend their civilization over all of North America was present in some of the most distinguished historians writing in the nineteenth century, including George Bancroft, John Lothrop Motley, William Hickling Prescott, and Francis Parkman.

> They believed that the national character was largely a
> matter of race, that liberty was the special attribute of
> the Germanic/Anglo-Saxon peoples, and that Providence
> had directed human progress westward to America
> where the United States was engaged in the fulfillment
> of a divine plan. (Horsman, 182–183)

Clearly one of the major causes for Hispanics being perceived by these Anglo-Saxon nationalists as inferior was the mixed European and Native American bloodline of the Hispanics in Mexico as well as in the Caribbean. Of course, the northern Europeans earlier on had indicted Spanish blood as inferior because of its infusion of Celtic, Jewish, and Moorish heritage, but miscegenation with the Indian "savages" was the greatest debilitator of their culture; it was another factor that justified their subjugation or replacement by the superior, pure Anglo-Saxons. A review article of Prescott's *Conquest of Mexico* in the *Massachusetts Quarterly Review* commented on the mixed-blood issue and concluded that an Anglo-Saxon would never mix "his proud blood, in stable wedlock with another race. There seems to be a natural antipathy to such unions with the black, or even the red, or yellow races of men—an antipathy almost peculiar to this remarkable tribe, the exterminator of other races."[20] If the superior race was not kept pure, then it would not maintain the necessary talents to rule and control lesser races. Nott wrote, "A great aim of philanthropy should be to keep the ruling races of the world as pure and as white as possible, for it is only through them that the others can be made prosperous and happy."[21] But Nott also repeated numerous times that it was the destiny of the whites to supplant the impure and colored races.

Despite this point of view, there were others that espoused limiting expansion precisely because the United States would be forced to incorporate inferior people into the Union, people who were inherently unfit for government or to be governed. Such was the rationale of New Englander George Perkins Marsh, who argued against the violent expansion of the Mexican War and against the acquisition of New Mexico and California: "they are inhabited by a mixed population, of habits, opinions, and characters incapable of sympathy or assimilation with our own; a race, whom the experience of an entire generation has proved to be unfitted for self-government, and unprepared to appreciate, sustain, or enjoy free institutions."[22]

And in truth, there were voices raised, mainly in the minority, that opposed expansionism and that did not accept the inherent superiority of an Anglo-Saxon race. In the North, particularly, the whole movement to abolish slavery generated a literature that countered the arguments of racial inferiority. Some fought expansionism as well as a tactic to forestall the extension of slavery to new territories and states. The annexation of both Texas and Cuba became caught up in this debate. Whatever saner, more humane objections were raised to the militant racial nationalism that infused the popular media and created a public opinion for expansionist government policies, the fact is that Manifest Destiny ruled the day and the Indians and the Hispanics paid for it in land and lives throughout much of the century.

Beginning in 1803, President Thomas Jefferson irrevocably set the course for U.S. expansion southward and westward by purchasing the Louisiana Territory for $15 million from France; Spain had ceded it to Napoleon through the Treaty of San Ildefonso in 1800. In 1804, much to Spain's consternation, Jefferson financed Lewis and Clark's expedition; the Spanish rightly foresaw this as a prelude to settlement of the territory by Anglos. In addition, Jefferson led Congress into passing the Mobile Act, which annexed into the Mississippi Territory all navigable waters, rivers, creeks, bays, and inlets that were located in the United States, were east of the Mississippi River, and emptied into the Gulf of Mexico.

In 1811, the U.S. Congress met in a secret session to approve a resolution declaring that the United States could not accept the passing of any part of the Floridas into the hands of a foreign power—that is, from Spain to France. It then passed enabling legislation to authorize the president to negotiate with local authorities an agreement, known as the "no-transfer resolution," to permit the United States to take custody of East Florida should it be threatened by a foreign power. This paved the way for the annexation of the Floridas by the United States, which actually happened after Andrew Jackson led a military force into Florida in 1819 and captured two Spanish forts. Via the Adams-Onís Treaty that same year, Spain was forced to sell the Florida Territory to the United States for $5 million as of 1821. The Adams-Onís Treaty established the border between the United States' Louisiana Territory and Spanish Texas at the Sabine River, following a latitude of 42 degrees all the way to the Pacific. The U.S. Congress ratified the Adams-Onís Treaty in 1821, the same year Mexico gained its independence from Spain and inherited an immense territory north of the Rio Grande River that had been organized up to then as the provinces of Texas, New Mexico, and Alta California. By the time Mexico had acquired its independence, permanent colonies existed in coastal California, southern Arizona, southern Texas, and in most of New Mexico and southern Colorado, more or less following the missionary trail outlined above.

Since the end of the eighteenth century, Spain had been subjected to an undeclared war by the United States, spurred on by the nascent doctrine of Manifest Destiny, which translated into rights of intervention and annexation and rights to colonize and use the soil. During successive interventions and encroachments, Spanish settlements and cities were occupied or taken over gradually by the United States: Baton Rouge in 1794, Mobile in 1811 and 1814 (as noted above), Amalia Island in 1813 and 1819, Penzacola in 1814 and 1818, San Marcos de Apalache in 1818. The South really became the first proving ground for this doctrine that would justify to Americans their later expansion westward. This undeclared war was carried out while Spain had its hands full with wars and rivalries with the ascendant French and British and with the independence movements of the Spanish colonies in the New World.

In 1822, President James Monroe recommended to Congress the recognition of the Spanish-American governments that had declared their independence from Spain: La Plata (Argentina), Chile, Peru, Gran Colombia, and Mexico. Monroe stated that these governments were entitled to recognition in order to protect them from European intervention; his statement, of course, prepared the way for the Monroe Doctrine, which officially reserved intervention rights in the Spanish-American republics for the United States. Monroe declared in 1823 that the Western Hemisphere was off limits to further European expansion and political ideology, and he guaranteed the independence of the Spanish-American countries.

That same year, U.S. Secretary of State John Quincy Adams informed the Spanish government that the annexation of Cuba would be indispensable to the Union's integrity. The United States had also exerted pressure on Simón Bolívar not to extend his liberation of the Americas to Cuba, which had sent numerous emissaries requesting the Liberator rid the island of the Spanish. U.S. designs on Cuba, which between 1838 and 1860 was the world's largest producer of sugar, continued throughout the century. In 1848, President James K. Polk made an offer to a very reluctant and incensed Spain to purchase Cuba for $100 million. President Franklin Pierce later increased the offer to $130 million and also warned that the United States might move to force Cuban independence from Spain in order to facilitate its annexation to the United States. Soon, much of the haggling over Cuba was suspended with the advent of the American Civil War. But the almost century-long pursuit of Cuba later culminated in the Spanish American War of 1898 and the island becoming a short-lived colony of the United States. The spoils of that war included Puerto Rico and Guam as the United States' first Pacific possessions. By the turn of the century, Manifest Destiny had brought the United States to the doorstep of Asia.

Anglo incursion into what would become the Southwest of the United States began in 1798 when a Yankee miner, Moses Austin, obtained a mining grant from the Spanish government for mining in the Missouri Territory. As a Spanish subject, he later applied for and was given an impresario grant to settle families in Texas. In March 1821, he was granted two hundred thousand acres on which to settle three hundred families. Moses Austin died before completing the settlement, and his son Stephen F. took over, bringing the first Anglo-American settlers onto land around the Lower Brazos River in Texas, which was now under the Mexican flag. The younger Austin renegotiated the agreement with Mexico, and by the end of the 1820s, some twenty thousand Anglo colonists were residing in Texas, six thousand of whom had been led by Austin. By the 1830s, the central government in Mexico was discouraging Anglo colonization and the Texas colonists, both Anglo and Mexican, were pursuing separation.

On April 21, 1836, Texas won its independence from Mexico by defeating and taking prisoner General Antonio López de Santa Anna at the Battle of San Jacinto. The victory of the Texans over the Mexicans was seen by Sam Houston and others—and passed down in Texas mythology as such—as the victory of the noble Anglo-Saxon race over the inferior Mexican rabble, despite Mexican colonists participating in and even leading some of the independence efforts. (In fact, Houston envisioned the Texas Republic pursuing its victory and conquering lands as far south as Panama: "The Texian standard of the single star, borne by the Anglo-Saxon race, shall display its bright folds in Liberty's triumph, on the isthmus of Darien."[23] Immediately after the war, Anglo-Texan feelings against Mexicans ran high, especially as they invoked the memory of massacres committed during the war at Goliad and at the Alamo. The numerically greater Anglos—some thirty thousand Anglos to four thou-

Antonio López de Santa Anna. Courtesy Library of Congress.

sand Mexicans in the new Republic (Meier and Rivera, 340)—persecuted the Mexicans and forced many off their lands and into Mexico. In the period of the Texas Republic and during statehood, Mexicans lost many of their land grants, quite often through illicit means, to the rapidly growing, land-hungry Anglo population. Quite often the justification for the land grabs was racial, and racially motivated policy in education and labor and other areas would come to characterize the life of Mexican Americans in Texas thereafter.

Anglo-Texas, following a manifest destiny of its own, also sought expansion at Mexico's expense. In 1841, Republic of Texas President Mirabeau Buonaparte Lamar sent an armed group of merchants to Santa Fe, New Mexico, to foment revolt against the Mexican government and promote union with the Texas Republic. The Santa Fe Expedition was ill-fated.

The three hundred Anglo- and Mexican-Texans, led by General Hugh McLeod, encountered hostile Indians and prairie fires and lost their way. Upon reaching New Mexico, they offered no resistance to Governor Manuel Armijo's soldiers, who took them prisoner.

On March 1, 1845, President John Tyler signed the resolution to annex Texas to the Union. Mexico severed its diplomatic relations with the United States, and as a result of a skirmish in disputed territory adjacent to the Rio Grande, the United States declared war on Mexico on May 13, 1846. The United States invaded Mexico under the banner of Manifest Destiny soon after the declaration of war, and General Winfield Scott marched to and took Mexico City, which surrendered on September 14, 1847. In 1846, Stephen Kearny's forces invaded New Mexico, and John C. Fremont merged his forces with Bear Flag rebels to take over the presidio in San Francisco, California. Under commodores John Sloat and Robert Stockton, the United States annexation of California was proclaimed on July 7, 1846. The United States defeated

Battle of Churubusco, Mexican War. Courtesy Library of Congress.

Battle of Monterey, Mexican War. Courtesy Library of Congress.

Mexico in 1848 and forced it to sign the Treaty of Guadalupe Hidalgo. During 1846 and 1847, there was much controversy in Congress and in the popular press as to the decision to annex all of Mexico to the United States. People were concerned about "debasing" the American form of government by making Mexico a colony and/or having its mongrelized people become citizens of the United States, so it was ultimately decided to incorporate only the more sparsely populated areas and use the Rio Grande and Gila Rivers as national boundaries. As Representative Edward C. Cabell of Florida stated, " ... if we annex the land, we must take the *population* along with it. And shall we, ... by an act of congress, convert the black, white, red, mongrel, miserable population of Mexico—the Mexicans, Indians, Mulattos, Mestizos, Chinos, Zambos, Quinteros—into free and enlightened American citizens, entitled to all the privileges which we enjoy?"[24]

Under the terms of the Treaty of Guadalupe Hidalgo, half of the land area of Mexico, including Texas, California, most of Arizona, and New Mexico, Utah, and Nevada, was ceded to the United States in exchange for peace and $18 million. The border between the United States and Mexico was set at the Gila and Rio Grande Rivers. Importantly for Mexican Americans—"Mexican Americans" was a new concept then—the treaty guaranteed their property, civil rights, and freedom of religion. The treaty also gave Mexican nationals one year to choose U.S. or Mexican citizenship. Seventy-five thousand Hispanic people chose to remain in the United States and become citizens by conquest. That same year, Mexico sent commissioners to Texas, New Mexico, and California to assist families in moving to Mexico as a result of these territories being ceded to the United States. The commissioners offered land and equipment to those willing to repatriate, but only three thousand chose to leave their lands and homes. Repatriation efforts were attempted again in 1855 and in the 1870s, including the offer of land in Sonora. Once more, the efforts only resulted in some two thousand Mexicans moving into Mexico.

When war was declared, Mexico had been a republic for just twenty-five years and was still recovering from two bloody wars, its war of independence and the war against Texas secession, while trying to define its nationhood and form its own governmental institutions. In addition, Mexico's first president under independence, Agustín de Iturbide, immediately declared himself emperor of Mexico in 1822. Forced to abdicate in 1823, he was followed by the disastrous dictator Antonio López de Santa Anna. *The American Whig Review* summarized what had led President Polk and the United States into the war and ultimate victory: "Mexico was poor, distracted, in anarchy, and almost in ruins—what could she do to stay the hand of our power, to impede the march of our greatness? We are Anglo-Saxon Americans; it was our 'destiny' to possess and to rule this continent—we were *bound* to it! We were a chosen people, and this our allotted inheritance, and we must drive out all other nations before us!"[25]

In the wake of the Mexican War, Mexicans in the Southwest experienced decades of oppression and persecution, quite often with the laws and authorities facilitating the expropriation of their lands, property, and civil rights. Squatting that broke up the old land grants and vigilantism that quite often resulted in the lynching of Mexicans characterized the decades before the turn of the century. Article 8 of the Treaty of Guadalupe Hidalgo guaranteed that the United States would protect the property rights of the population of the Southwest. However, the United States disregarded this and other provisions of the treaty, and Mexican Americans and their property were put at the mercy of a political, economic, and legal system that was completely foreign to them. As hordes of land-hungry "pioneers" and entrepreneurs descended on the Southwest, the Mexican Americans fell victim to legal manipulations, fraud, and outright theft.

> Congress could have authenticated titles to land grants
> in the Southwest that were occupied at the time of the
> American occupation. Or it could have required the
> government to bear costs of litigation essential to
> settling land grant titles. Instead it forced claimants to
> Spanish and Mexican land grants to appear before
> courts and commissions staffed by Anglo American
> judges and commissioners unfamiliar with the Spanish
> language and with Spanish and Mexican land law.
> Mexican American landholders were forced to hire
> expensive Anglo American lawyers, and carry on com-
> plicated and prolonged litigation, often lasting for
> twenty years or more, before a final legal decision was
> secured. ... The burden of proving that their land grant

77

titles were legal was simply beyond the power of most Mexican American landowners. At the mercy of a complex, expensive legal system and of greedy, often corrupt, Anglo American lawyers, politicians, government officials, surveyors and judges, they lost most of their land grants. (Rivera and Meier, 187)

In California, a particularly outrageous collusion between the state legislature, the railroads seeking right-of-way, the banks, and the squatters functioned to expropriate many of the land grants. After the Mexican War, the increasing number of immigrants to California put pressure on the federal and state governments to question the validity of land grants and to support squatters' rights. California congressmen sought to create legal means to invalidate the Mexican and Spanish land grants and prevailed upon the U.S. Congress to pass the Land Act of 1851, which required land grant holders to prove their ownership before a Board of Land Commissioners in San Francisco between 1852 and 1856. During this period, an estimated two-fifths of the Californio ranchers lost the rights to their lands due to, among other reasons, a combination of corrupt commissioners, unscrupulous lawyers, and their inability to pay lawyers. The loss of the ranchers' lands meant a loss of their economic base and way of life.

In 1856, Pablo de la Guerra addressed the California state senate, which was predominantly made up of Anglo-Americans, requesting the repeal of the unjust laws that supported squatters:

[The Californios] are the conquered who lay prostate before the conqueror and ask for his protection in the enjoyment of the little which their fortune has left them. They are the ones who had been sold like sheep—those who were abandoned and sold by Mexico. They do not understand the language which is now spoken in their own country. They have no voice in this Senate, except

such as I am now weakly speaking on their behalf. ... I
have seen old men of sixty and seventy years of age
weeping like children because they have been cast out
of their ancestral home. They have been humiliated and
insulted. They have been refused the privilege of taking
water from their own wells. They have been refused the
privilege of cutting their own firewood. ... Any impartial
party who would examine the law would see that it
protects the squatter, and rightly or wrongly displaces
the owner of his equal rights—rights which are invio-
lable according to human and divine law.[26]

The brunt of the law's support of squatters was faced
by the wealthier Californios, many of whom had supported
annexation to the United States and looked forward to prosperity and respect under the new regime. They soon became disillusioned, and a tone of nostalgia and regret came
to characterize many of their memoirs and writings well into
the twentieth century. In her impassioned novel, *The Squatter and the Don,* María Amparo Ruiz de Burton amply illustrated the undoing of the great *rancherías* and the
disintegration of culture and family that often attended this
disruption of a traditional lifestyle. "I think but few Americans know or believe to what extent we have been wronged
by Congressional action," Ruiz de Burton lamented. "And
truly, I believe that Congress itself did not anticipate the
effect of its laws upon us, and how we could be despoiled,
we the conquered people." (Ruiz de Burton, 67)

Another writer, Guadalupe Vallejo, from one of the leading Californio families whose lands were lost, recalled nos-
talgically the days before the coming of the Anglos:

It seems to me that there never was a more peaceful or
happy people on the face of the earth than the Spanish,
Mexican, and Indian population of Alta California before
the American conquest. We were the pioneers of the

79

> Pacific coast, building towns and Missions while General
> Washington was carrying on the war of the Revolution,
> and we often talk together of the days when a few
> hundred large Spanish ranches and Mission tracts
> occupied the whole country from the Pacific to the San
> Joaquin. No class of American citizens is more loyal
> than the Spanish Californians, but we shall always be
> especially proud of the traditions and memories of the
> long pastoral age before 1840. (Vallejo, 183)

One of the premises of Manifest Destiny, as mentioned previously, was that the lands to the west and south were unpopulated. Mexicans and Indians were absent from the mythical landscape, and this misconception can still be seen today in many motion picture representations of the West. In an effort to populate these lands and secure their resources for the national good, Congress passed the Homestead Act in 1862, which further allowed squatters to claim and settle vacant lands. Often, the lands claimed already belonged to Mexican Americans.

The lands, however, were not the only properties being contested as the Anglos moved west. The rights to exploit natural resources were also appropriated. This was the case, for example, of the salt mines located one hundred miles east of El Paso that had been used by the local population for generations: They were suddenly appropriated by one Samuel Maverick in 1866. In 1867, Anglo-Republican politicians then tried to form a monopoly on the salt mines, thus causing the dispute of the local populace with Maverick to escalate into riots, looting, and deaths: the El Paso Salt War lasted for more than a decade. The trade routes pioneered by Mexicans were also contested: In 1857, Anglo businessmen in South Texas attempted to run off Mexican teamsters from the profitable business that Mexicans had built up for generations. Known as the Cart War, the dispute eventually resulted in some seventy-five deaths. The California gold rush, in particular, ushered in a period of lawlessness and ruthlessness that inflicted great damage on the civilian population of California. And Anglos targeted Mexicans, who had long experience in mining gold fields, for persecution within and outside of the law.

Outside of the law, in 1849 numerous Mexicans were expelled from the California gold fields by vigilante groups. Within the law, the first California assembly asked the U.S. Congress to bar all foreigners from the mines—through a law selectively used against Mexicans or Mexican Americans—no distinction was made. And then in 1850, the California legislature passed the Foreign Miners Tax Law, which levied a charge of $20 per month on anyone who was not a U.S. citizen. Because it was difficult to collect the tax, as well as to protect those who had paid it, it was largely disregarded. This led to increased violence against Mexicans by Anglo vigilantes, who once again found an affinity for lynching. In 1851, the tax was repealed, but by then most of the Hispanics had been driven from the mines. Also within the law was the California Anti-Vagrancy Act of 1855, known too as the Greaser Law because it specifically targeted "greasers" for its application. The Anti-Vagrancy Act set about restricting the freedoms and civil rights of Mexican Americans, including such cultural pastimes as cockfighting and bullfighting. The act was a legal reflection of the widespread anti-Mexican/anti-Hispanic sentiments current in Anglo society in California.

As Mexicans and Mexican Americans abandoned ranches, mines, and other businesses, the period from the end of the Mexican War to the early twentieth century consequently was characterized by the creation of a class of landless Mexican Americans who eventually became the cowboys, farmhands, mine workers and wage earners in the employ of Anglo-Americans. It was also a period of open revolt by Mexican Americans who formed guerrilla and separatist movements, such as the Cortina War, or pursued the life of outlaws in rejection of the legal and political system that had marginalized them and made them destitute.

The Cortina War, named for upper-class Texas rancher and bandit-social revolutionary Juan Nepomuceno Cortina, began in 1859 when Cortina and a group of volunteers attempting to redress Anglo oppression of Texas Mexicans captured Brownsville, Texas. They raised the Mexican flag and issued a list of grievances that especially focused on Anglo mistreatment of Mexicans and Mexican Americans. In conflicts and confrontations that followed with the U.S. Army under Robert E. Lee, the Texas Rangers, and local militia, Cortina issued one proclamation after another in pursuit of social justice. In the mid-1860s, Cortina began making a life for himself in government and in the military in northern Mexico, fighting against French intervention. During the American Civil War, he was an active anti-Confederate and, after the war, a pardon was sought for him by Union factions. When this failed, he lived out his life in Mexico, spending his last years in prison in Mexico City for falling out of favor with the ruling powers. In his first proclamation, issued in English and Spanish on broadsides in 1859, Cortina laid claim to a just cause:

> Our object, as you have seen, has been to chastise the villainy of our enemies, which heretofore has gone unpunished. These have connived with each other, and form, so to speak, a perfidious inquisitorial lodge to prosecute and rob us, without any cause, and for no other crime on our part than that of being of Mexican origin, considering us, doubtless, destitute of those gifts which they themselves do not possess.[27]

Texas Rangers displaying bandits they killed.
Courtesy Archives Division, Texas State Library.

In his second proclamation of 1859, Cortina demonstrated the rhetorical talents and firebrand passion that made him a leader of men in his sometimes quixotic attempts to right social and political injustices:

> Mexicans! When the state of Texas began to receive the new organization which its sovereignty required as an integrant part of the Union, flocks of vampires, in the guise of men, came and scattered themselves in the settlements, without any capital except the corrupt heart and the most perverse intentions. Some, brimful of laws, pledged to us their protection against the attacks of the rest; ... while others, to the abusing of our unlimited confidence, when we entrusted them with our titles, which secured the future of our families, refused to return them under false and frivolous pretexts. ... Many of you have been robbed of your property, incarcerated, chased, murdered, and hunted like wild beasts, because your labor was fruitful, and because your industry excited the vile avarice which led them. ...

83

>   Mexicans! My part is taken; the voice of revelation
> whispers to me that to me is entrusted the work of
> breaking the chains of your slavery.[28]

The oral lore is replete with examples of mines stolen, Mexican miners lynched, and the civilian population subjected to atrocities. "El Corrido de Joaquín Murieta" (The Ballad of Joaquín Murieta) is a long, lyric boast in the first person that reveals how social injustice led Mexicans and Mexican Americans beyond the law and even to strike out at society as a whole, or particularly Anglo-American society. According to the ballad (ca. 1850), the infamous Murieta's life as a bandit began as vengeance for the claim jumpers who stole his mine and killed his wife and brother:

Famed California "bandit" Joaquín Murieta. Courtesy Library of Congress.

>   *Cuando apenas era un niño*
>   *huérfano a mí me dejaron*
>   *sin que me hiciera un cariño*
>   *a mi hermano lo mataron*
>   *a mi esposa Carmelita*
>   *cobardes la asesinaron.*
>
>   *Ahora salgo a los caminos*
>   *A matar a americanos*
>   *"Tú fuistes el promotor*
>   *De la muerte de mi hermano*
>   *Lo agarrastes indefenso*
>   *Desgraciado americano."*

84

A los ricos y avarientos
Yo les quité su dinero
A los humildes y pobres
Yo me quitaba el sombrero
Ay, qué leyes tan injustas
Voy a darme a bandolero. [29]

[When I was just a child
I was left an orphan
without time for even a last caress of me
they killed my brother
and my wife too
the cowards killed her.

Now I go out on the highways
to kill Americans
"You are the reason
for the death of my brother.
You took him defenseless,
You unholy American."

Of the rich and greedy
I relieve them of their money.
To the humble and poor
I take off my hat.
Oh, what unjust laws,
I give myself to the bandit life.]

Another famous California bandit, Tiburcio Vásquez, similarly stressed the vengeance motive in launching his life as an outlaw:

My career grew out of the circumstances by which I was surrounded as I grew into manhood. I was in the habit of attending balls and parties given by the native Californians, into which the Americans, then beginning to become numerous, would force themselves and shove the native-born men aside, monopolizing the dances and the women. This was about 1852.

A spirit of hatred and revenge took possession of me. I had numerous fights in defense of what I believed to be my rights and those of my countrymen. The officers were continuously in pursuit of me. I believe that we were unjustly and wrongfully deprived of the social rights which belonged to us. So perpetually was I involved in these difficulties that I at length determined to leave the thickly-settled portion of the country, and did so.[30]

California outlaw Tiburcio Vásquez. Courtesy Arte Público Press.

In 1853, the United States sought to round out its southwestern border for construction of the transcontinental railroad and arranged to purchase for $10 million the Mesilla Valley from Mexico, constituting some twenty-nine million acres that would become the southernmost parts of Arizona and New Mexico. The U.S. minister to Mexico, James Gadsden, attempted to force Mexico's cession of five border states and Baja California by sending two thousand U.S. troops to the New Mexico border. The Gadsden Treaty, which went into effect in 1854, was signed with the infamous President Antonio López de Santa Anna, who feared another large-scale U.S. intervention or Texas-style revolt inspired by the United States. On December 30, 1853, Santa

Antonio Lopez de Santa Anna. Courtesy Library of Congress.

Anna signed the treaty and to this day in Mexico is known as the "vende-patrias," seller of the homeland. Because of the treaty, hundreds of Mexicans who had relocated out of the Southwest in the aftermath of the Mexican War once again found themselves in the United States. One balladeer from New Mexico warned his compatriots of the coming of the Anglos in "Corrido de los Americanos" (Ballad of the Americans):

Voy a hablar del extranjero
y lo que digo es verdad,
quieren tenernos de esclavos,
pero eso no les valdrá.

Señores, pongan cuidado
a la raza americana,
vienen a poseer las tierras,
las que les vendió Santa Ana.
....
Vienen dándole al cristiano
y haciéndole al mundo guerra,
vienen a echarnos del país
y a hacerse de nuestra tierra. (In Castañeda, 226–227)

[I'm going to talk about foreigners
and what I say is the truth,
they want us as their slaves,
but they won't have their way.

People, be careful
of the American race,
they come to take possession of the land,
the ones sold to them by Santa Anna.
....
They come singing of Christianity
and making war on the world,
they're coming to throw us out of our country
and to take our land.]

87

Land and property were not the only rights under attack by the Anglo-Americans in their takeover of the Southwest. Language and culture—the Mexicans' very identity—which were also protected by the Treaty of Guadalupe Hidalgo, were also at risk. From one year to the next, in the transition from Mexican to U.S. dominion, the official language changed in many places, as did the judicial and political systems. Almost every facet of public life had been transformed. The Catholic Church, now, also saw competition from the Protestant religions brought by the Anglo settlers. The mounting racism that originally had justified Anglo expansion also extended to the use of the Spanish language and the entire culture of the Spanish speakers. As noted by a Laredo poet, Santiago de la Hoz, in 1904, the very identity of Mexicans was threatened:

> *¡Pueblo despierta ya! Tus hijos crecen*
> *Y una herencia de oprobio no merecen,*
> *Vuelve en ti de esa locura insana:*
> *¡Si siguen criando siervos tantas madres,*
> *Tus hijos, los esclavos de mañana,*
> *Renegarán el nombre de sus padres! (In Castañeda, 25–26)*

> *[People, wake up now! Your children grow older*
> *And do not deserve a heritage of oppression,*
> *Come out of that unhealthy insanity:*
> *If so many mothers raise servile children,*
> *Your children, the slaves of tomorrow,*
> *Will deny their parents' names!]*

An editorial writer, José González, in the December 30, 1904, issue of New Mexico's *El Labrador* newspaper felt the need to defend the Spanish language in the face of the cultural and linguistic onslaught. This assault had persisted in the Southwest since the Mexican War and had periodically became intensified with nativist crusades, such as today's English-Only movement:

Se ha hecho moda aquí en Nuevo México tratar con una especie de vituperio y menosprecio no solamente a los que hablan español sino al idioma mismo, cual si aquéllos fuesen culpables de algún delito con hablar la lengua que heradaron de sus antepasados y como si ésta no fuese uno de los idiomas modernos más apreciados y mejor perfeccionados que se hablan en Europa y en América. Se pretende y se quiere exigir que todo el pueblo nativo de Nuevo México sepa el idioma nacional, que es el inglés, aún sabiendo que esto ha sido imposible por razón de que no hemos tenido los medios ni las facilidades para aprenderlo. Aun comprendiendo esto no faltan muchos que quieran que el español sea un idioma proscrito y que aquéllos que lo hablan sean despojados de sus franquicias y de sus derechos.[31]

[It has become fashionable here in New Mexico to treat with a kind of reproach and contempt not only those who speak Spanish, but the language itself. It is as if they were guilty of some crime in speaking the language which came down from their forefathers, and as if it is not one of the most respected and best perfected of modern languages that is spoken in Europe and America. They try to demand that all the native people of New Mexico know the national language, which is English, though knowing this has been impossible because we have not had the means or the facilities to learn it. Even knowing this, there has been no lack of those who want Spanish to be a prohibited language, and those who speak it to be despoiled of their franchises and rights of citizenship.]

Because of the numerical superiority of the Mexican population in New Mexico, admission to statehood was continuously denied to the territory until 1912, whereas the California territory achieved statehood as early as 1850. In 1850, the U.S. Congress passed a series of laws, known as the Compromise of 1850, to defer the divisiveness of the slavery issue. After the Mexican War, Texas and the other territories of the Southwest pursued admission to the Union as states, but this further complicated the issue of slavery, as debate ensued as to whether they would individually enter as "free" or "slave" states. Also complicating the issue was the fact that New Mexico and southern Texas were populated predominantly by Mexicans. The compromise had California being admitted as a state and New Mexico remaining a territory. Texas was given $10,000 to compensate for part of its territory east of the Rio Grande River ceded to New Mexican territory. The New Mexicans were especially disappointed by the denial of statehood. But the fear in the U.S. Congress of having inferior races as citizens and legislators was considerable.

Typical of the statements in opposition to New Mexican statehood were Florida Senator James D. Westcott's, who did not want to be "compelled to receive not merely the white citizens of California and New Mexico, but the peons, negroes, and Indians of all sorts, the wild tribe of Comanches, the bug-and-lizard-eating 'Diggers,' and other half-monkey savages in those countries, *as equal citizens of the United States.*" [32]

Resistance to extending citizenship to peoples of other races had come early on in Congress from both the Whig and Democratic parties. Such statements as: "I do not want any mixed races in our union, nor men of any color except white, unless they be slaves. Certainly not as voters or legislators ... ."[33] typified congressional sentiment. This attitude explains somewhat the policies set for facilitating settlement of Anglo-Americans in the West and resisting New Mexico's statehood until Anglos were in controlling majority of the territory.

The slavery issue also determined the direction of the discussion over annexation of Cuba and its eventual statehood.

In 1854, as mentioned previously, President Franklin Pierce offered Spain $130 million for the island and threatened U.S. support of the Cuban independence movement in what is known as the Ostend Manifesto, presented by U.S. representatives at Aix-la-Chapelle, France. This declaration brought a hostile reaction against U.S. imperialism from the European powers and caused Spain to resist the U.S. initiatives even more strenuously. But in the United States, the debate over Cuba was yet more complicated in that southern congressmen were hoping to add another "slave" state to the Union. The Civil War put these initiatives to rest for a period. Nevertheless, U.S. expansionism under Manifest Destiny was striking out in all directions and even was directed as far south as Nicaragua in 1856, when U.S. citizen William Walker seized the presidency of Nicaragua and made English the official language of the country. Once again, it was President Franklin Pierce who, during his reelection bid, exploited feelings about slavery and Manifest Destiny and officially recognized Walker's short-lived government. After Pierce was not nominated by his party at the Democratic convention, he withdrew what came to be an increasingly embarrassing and blatantly imperialistic recognition of Walker's government.

But with the annexation of the territories and states of the Southwest, the United States had indeed made it to the sea, to be sure at the expense of Mexicans and Indians who, as the ideology of Manifest Destiny had predicted, had to surrender their space to a superior and divinely favored race. Horsman argues that it was the very confrontation with Mexicans that had led Anglo-Saxons to see themselves as a race:

> By the 1830's the Americans were eagerly grasping at reasons for their own success and for the failure of others. Although the white Americans of Jacksonian

91

America wanted personal success and wealth, they also wanted a clear conscience. If the United States was to remain in the minds of the people a nation divinely ordained for great deeds, then the fault of the suffering inflicted in the rise to power and prosperity had to lie elsewhere. White Americans could rest easier if the suffering of other races could be blamed on racial weakness rather than on the whites' relentless search for wealth and power. In the 1830's and 1840's, when it became obvious that American and Mexican interests were incompatible and that Mexicans would suffer, innate weaknesses were found in the Mexicans. Americans, it was argued, were not to be blamed for forcibly taking the northern provinces of Mexico, for Mexicans, like Indians, were unable to make proper use of the land. The Mexicans had failed because they were a mixed, inferior race with considerable Indian and some black blood. The world would benefit if a superior race shaped the future of the Southwest. (Horsman, 210)

It is in this period that many of the stereotypes of Mexicans are solidified in the literature of travelers, pioneers, and later politicians and policymakers as well as in the popular entertainments and media, such as the dime novel. Mexicans were pictured as a mongrel race, cowardly, cruel, lazy, superstitious, and shiftless, which of course was an inheritance of the stereotypes created in the Black Legend. As Horsman notes, the process of dehumanizing the people who would be misused and destroyed rapidly preceded the expropriation of their lands. (Horsman, 211)

The next Hispanics to become subjects of U.S. expansionism resided close to the borders of the United States: in the Caribbean. The relationship between the Spanish colonies in the Caribbean and the British colonies of New England actually began in the sixteenth century as a by-product of war and competition between England and Spain. The

Spanish colonies from that time were plagued by attacks and had various of their port cities occupied by the British navy and privateers—by the likes of Francis Drake both as pirate and privateer. It must also be remembered that natives of Cuba, and to a lesser extent Puerto Rico, have resided since the 1560s in territories that are now part of the United States in such areas as St. Augustine, Florida.

The rudiments of an illicit trade between the Hispanic and British colonies began when Spanish-American goods and merchants ended up in New England. In 1670, Spain and England finally abated some of the competition with one another upon signing an accord that recognized each other's presence in the Caribbean: the Treaty of Madrid. The treaty further sanctioned England's holdings in the Americas. But trade between the Spanish and British colonies was only permitted with a special license; this restricted commerce severely and led to the development of smuggling between their colonies. Then, later, England became a major supplier of slaves to the Americas, even to the Spanish colonies. In 1717, England's South Sea Company obtained permission to bring 144,000 African slaves into the Spanish colonies at a rate of forty-eight hundred per year for thirty years. The trade rapidly expanded and grew into an additional link in the economies, especially in Cuba and southern plantation states of the United States in the nineteenth century.

During the Seven Years War, the British occupied Havana for ten months. Cubans came into contact with soldiers and traders from the British colonies in North America and discovered the benefits of commercial trade outside of the Spanish Empire. This was to have great influence on the future of Cuban-U.S. relations, especially on trading. During the first half of the nineteenth century, the trading relationship expanded dramatically, leading as well to the beginning of the

Cuban communities in New Orleans, Philadelphia, and New York. Also, many Cubans began coming to the United States to pursue their education, and the country became a refuge for Cuban dissidents, exiles, and revolutionaries plotting the independence of their homeland. Many Cubans also furthered the idea of annexation of Cuba to the United States, and both annexationists and revolutionaries continuously prevailed upon U.S. leadership to support and underwrite separation from Spain. But even the revolutionaries seeking independence foresaw a close relationship with the United States in governing their own republic.

The roots of such Spanish-American revolutionary foment on U.S. soil were planted during the American Revolution when the liberal ideas of the founding fathers found their way into the Spanish colonies in the Americas, inspiring their own movements. Then, too, there was direct participation by Hispanics in the American Revolution, and Hispanics were already living in New England during the early days of the Republic. New York, Philadelphia, and New Orleans became seats where Hispanic expatriate communities took in the ideas of "life, liberty and the pursuit of happiness," and sought to set the courses of their nations based on the successful model of the nascent United States. One of the first of these activists to launch a revolutionary movement from American soil was the Venezuelan soldier Francisco de Miranda. As a soldier in the Spanish army, he had participated in the War of Independence of the thirteen British colonies in North America, and he had also participated in the French Revolution. In 1806, Miranda tried to liberate Venezuela by embarking from New York on an ill-fated liberation mission with a group of two hundred soldiers. Later, Miranda joined forces with Simón Bolívar.

94

From the turn of the nineteenth century, New York and Philadelphia in particular developed substantial expatriate communities from Spain (during the Napoleonic intervention), the Caribbean, Mexico, and South America. These people raised funds, published political treatises, translated Thomas Paine and other founders of American republicanism, and published scores of combatively liberal newspapers[34] that they circulated throughout Hispanic communities in North America, Mexico, and the Caribbean. Clearly, the most numerous and active among these expatriates were the Cubans, and a good deal of nineteenth-century-Cuban history, most notably its theoretical basis for independence from Spain, was developed on U.S. soil. In addition, numerous military expeditions were financed by Hispanics in the United States and were launched from U.S. ports.

Spanish Americans in the United States, especially Cubans, took advantage of anti-Spanish sentiments in the Anglo-American population—the result of the Spanish Black Legend—to persuade and influence U.S. policymakers to intervene in favor of Cuba's separation from Spain. Some of the most notable revolutionary polemicists and creative writers insistently recalled the atrocities committed against the Indians and added a new list of Spanish transgressions in Cuba and the Caribbean. Poets in exile published their verse in the Spanish-language newspapers and in such anthologies as *El laúd del desterrado* (The Lute of the Exiled, 1856)[35] and, despite being pure-blooded Spanish Creoles, these liberals cast and otherwise identified themselves with the nearly extinct Taínosíno Indians of the Caribbean.

Cuba's great philosopher, theologian, and newspaper editor (founder and publisher of the first exile newspaper, *El Habanero,* in the 1820s), Félix Varela, spent the better part of his career in exile in Philadelphia and New

95

York. He became the Catholic Church's first vicar of the diocese of New York, anonymously published what is the first historical novel ever written in the Spanish language, *Jicoténcal* (the name of an Tlaxcalan Indian prince),[36] and openly sided with the Tlaxcalans and Aztecs and attacked Spanish cruelty and treachery. In applying the Black Legend against the Spanish as a lever to secure independence from Spain, the Cubans were not alone. Spanish Americans throughout the Southern Hemisphere were doing the same. However, the Cubans, Puerto Ricans, and others were revolting from within the bosom of a society that had been nurtured on such anti-Spanish propaganda and that was employing it to justify its own imperialistic expansion.

As Cuba became the world's largest producer of sugar in the nineteenth century, and southern states were anxious to increase the number of "slave" states, American designs on Cuba intensified and led to, as mentioned previously, various attempts by the United States to purchase the island from Spain. Also, after a partial reconciliation with Spain in the 1850s, the Cuban revolutionary movement once again gained strength for another thirty years, causing a surge in immigration to the United States corresponding with their wars—the Ten Years' War (1868–1878) and the Independence War (1895–1898)—and the growth of the cigar industry in Florida, Louisiana, and New York.[37] Beginning in the 1860s, a large segment of the tobacco industry relocated from Cuba to the United States to get around the U.S. protectionist tariffs and to avoid the turbulence of the wars of independence and a very active labor movement. In addition, the factories now would be closer to the primary markets.

At the same time, Cuba was attracting large U.S. investments in its agriculture. In 1890, the McKinley Tariff practically curtailed cigar shipments from Cuba to the United

States and benefited even more the Cuban cigar industry located within the United States.[38] By 1895, the year of the outbreak of the final phase of the Cuban independence war, North Americans had invested $50 million dollars in Cuba, and trade amounted to over $100 million per year. (Leonard, 183) Following the election of William McKinley in 1897, yellow journalism promoted U.S. intervention in Cuba on behalf of its independence by invoking every anti-Spanish slur and racial attack that had been passed on through the Black Legend and Manifest Destiny. Publishers William Randolph Hearst and Joseph Pulitzer built up such an Hispanophobic frenzy through the press that preachers directed their sermons against Spain, anti-Spanish demonstrations were held by Princeton University students and Leadville miners, and the Youngstown, Ohio, Chamber of Commerce even boycotted the Spanish onion! (Horsman, 122–123) To further promote Hispanophobia, a new edition of Las Casas's *Brief Relation* was published in 1898 under the inflammatory title, *An Historical and True Account of the Cruel Massacre and Slaughter of 20,000,000 People in the West Indies by the Spaniards.*

The U.S. Congress declared war on Spain on March 19, 1898. After much of the war had already been fought and won by Cuban insurgents, the United States conducted negotiations with Spain without the Cubans, forcing Spain through the Treaty of Paris, signed December 12, 1898, to relinquish its dominion over Cuba, Puerto Rico, the Virgin Islands, Guam, and the Philippines.

In effect, these islands had unwittingly traded one colonial ruler for another. In one fell swoop, the United States became the colonial empire that had been warned against and avoided earlier in the century; it would govern the various and disparate races that had been feared earlier. In 1898 Hawaii also became a protectorate of the United States. The objections to governing territories that were filled with "black, mixed, degraded, and ignorant, or inferior races" had lost out to more important geopolitical concerns and trade issues. The ideological line, however, that covered this change from expanding borders to appropriation of the colonial model, was that the United States had a moral obligation to extend the benefits of Anglo-Saxon culture to the backward areas of the world. And, there was an added imperial goal for dominion over the Caribbean islands: the impending construction of a trans-isthmian canal in Central America, a canal that had been discussed and negotiated for half a century. The last piece in the puzzle that made the United States into a colonial power in Spanish America was Panama. It was added—although not as a star on the U.S. flag, none of these colonies became stars—after the United States fomented Panama's revolution and separation from Colombia in 1903 to acquire better control of the intended canal zone along with better terms for lease of the zone, all the while staving off British and other European interests by invoking the Monroe Doctrine.

Thus, the United States went into the twentieth century with its own military government in place in Cuba and Puerto Rico, and it was poised for numerous military interventions in the Caribbean, Mexico, and Central America in the name of the Monroe Doctrine and a soon-to-be-added corollary to the Monroe Doctrine by President Theodore Roosevelt. Americans felt obliged to extend the benefits of Anglo-American freedom and liberty to "inferior" peoples, who had such a difficult time governing themselves. Throughout the century, the numerous interventions in the internal politics of Santo Domingo, Mexico, and Central America favored and protected U.S. business interests in these countries and extended the power and control of the United States over their economies. (Puerto Ricans became citizens of the United States in 1907 under the Jones Act and lived under U.S. military government until 1953; Cuba became nominally independent and elected its own president in 1901, but through the Platt Amendment forced into its constitution by the United States, Cuba was compelled to accept United States intervention at any time.) Part of the relationship that developed with this new, expanded sphere in the Hispanic world was that of sender countries (suppliers of labor and other raw materials) and the receiver (the United States as a grand labor market and manufacturing power). Immigrant labor, both legal and illegal, became fully instituted in the relationship of the United States with Mexico and the Hispanic peoples of the Caribbean.

During the twentieth century, further expansionism would come through trade and investment, not territorial expansion, and it would always be protected by the "big stick": gunboat and dollar diplomacy. In the twentieth century, the moral imperative of the Anglo-American empire became the incorporation and maintenance of the Spanish-American countries within the U.S. economic and political sphere. Meanwhile, the United States fashioned an immigration policy that treated the "inferior" races of these societies as the unskilled power to develop the agribusiness and manufacturing industries at home so as to further elaborate the economic miracle that was the United States. In essence, the greatest resources that Mexico, Puerto Rico, and to some extent Cuba, had to offer the United States were the low-wage laborers that would be needed to supplant that great institution that had enriched the South: slavery. During times of war, also, the resident Hispanic workers and their children—and the entire male citizenry of Puerto Rico—would make an excellent noncommissioned fighting force.

Chapter Four

IMMIGRATION
POLICY ❖ ❖ ❖

BY THE TURN OF THE CENTURY, the Spanish Black Legend and
the doctrine of Manifest Destiny had done much to fix and
reinforce in the American mind the stereotypes of Hispanics as an inferior, mongrelized race. However, American immigration and employment policies and practices in the
twentieth century also defined Hispanics as lower-class,
unskilled workers fit to do the types of arduous, low-wage
labor that European immigrants and Anglo-Americans were
unwilling or unable to do. In addition, because of the proximity of Mexico and the Caribbean to the United States and
their poverty, political instability, and economic dependence
on their northern neighbor, theirs was a ready source of
labor. U.S. businesses, often with the support of both their
own and the Spanish-American governments, fashioned programs and practices that discouraged settlement by these
workers in the United States, but cultivated them as temporary labor that could be employed in times of war and economic expansion, when labor was scarce. But during times
of recession and depression, they saw Hispanics as a labor
pool that could be returned to the sender countries. These
policies and practices developed when there were enormous

political and economic factors pushing laborers out of the sender countries and equally strong economic factors pulling them into the United States, resulting in massive immigration during this century.

U.S. immigration policy as it developed and was applied to Hispanics in Mexico, the Caribbean, and Central America over the twentieth century was quite unlike that created to facilitate the settling of the vast land mass of the United States with Europeans during the nineteenth century. U.S. policy encouraged the immigration of masses of working-class Hispanics for employment at the lowest levels in agribusiness and basic industries and ultimately as service workers in both domestic and public spheres. Much of the immigrant flow grew to bear a specific and intimate relationship with U.S. foreign policy as it affected the sender nations.

As U.S. business interests extended to and developed in the Spanish-American countries, and as the United States became involved in the internal politics of those countries, Hispanic labor became a commodity that could also be imported along with other raw materials and products. But then, too, the myth or reputation of the economic opportunities and political freedoms available in the United States spread widely from mouth to mouth in the sender countries. Also, it became preferable for many Hispanic workers in the second half of the century to pursue temporary employment in the United States rather than abandon their homeland completely. The Mexican-American border was completely porous with back-and-forth traffic, as were the air routes to and from the Northeastern Seaboard for Puerto Ricans, Cubans, and even Dominicans. But the Puerto Ricans had the added advantage over other Hispanics in that they were U.S. citizens and had rights of freedom of passage.

Dominicans often entered the United States through Puerto Rico and traveled just as freely.

While most immigration policy developed in the United States has been restrictive in nature, it was not until the twentieth century that any restrictions at all were placed upon Hispanics. Given the technology and resources available in the past century, it would have been almost impossible to enforce any restrictions on crossing a recently created border with Mexico. Then, too, the vast expanses of arid land also served as barriers to travel before railroads and highways existed. With the exception of the unenforced Alien Act of 1798, almost all immigration was unrestricted during the nineteenth century, when the United States was eager to cement its claim on its newly acquired territories and states by settling them and developing their natural resources. In addition, the right of American employers to recruit and hire foreign contract laborers was established in 1864 during wartime, and the practice continued until 1885, when the practice was banned by the Alien Labor Act; however, it laid the foundation for practices that would be resumed later. (Briggs, 97) The only racial or ethnic restrictions on immigration were those instituted in 1882 against the Chinese and in 1907 and 1924 against the Japanese. The other restrictions generally dealt with disqualifying criminals, political radicals, the mentally ill, etc. (Mitchell, 11)

During and after World War I, a great deal of anti-European sentiment developed in the United States, and limits began to be imposed in the form of a quota system, mainly directed at southern and eastern Europeans who after 1890 had become the predominant immigrants from Europe. Through laws passed in 1921, 1924, and 1929, sending nations were assigned a yearly quota of immigrant visas that could be issued, with an annual ceiling of 150,000 immigrants fixed for quota nations. All independent states in the Western Hemisphere were exempt from the quota system and therefore most of the regulation. The European tide was stemmed, with immigration falling from 60 percent prior to 1920 to less than 30 percent during the ensuing decade. (Divine, chapter 1)

Massive Mexican immigration to the United States began after 1880 as the railroads were built both in the Southwest and in Mexico, and the southwestern economy began to build up. From 1880 to 1900, approximately 127,000 Mexicans entered the United States, one and one-third times the native Mexican population in the Southwest in 1848. (Rosales, 32) The period from the turn of the century to 1929, however, saw the greatest outpouring of Mexican labor so far. Employers in the Southwest, and later in the Midwest, created a system to recruit and transport Mexican laborers from the interior and the border to build and maintain railroads; to staff the Chicago stockyards; to work in

Recruitment center for braceros in San Antonio. Courtesy Library of Congress.

Migrant farm workers. Courtesy Library of Congress.

the open hearth of steel mills in Gary, Indiana, East Chicago, South Chicago, and Bethlehem, Pennsylvania; to plant sugar beets in Colorado, Wyoming, and Montana; and tend to the crops in Minnesota, Michigan, and Washington State.

The primary factor motivating Mexican emigration was the violent disruption of life and the country's economic base caused by the Mexican Revolution. The high levels of unemployment, the low wages, and the heritage of rural peonage made the Mexican laborers attractive, especially for employment in agriculture. The factors pulling Mexican labor to the United States, from the border to as far north as Buffalo, New York, and Washington State were the transformation of the Southwest, especially Texas and California, to the seats of a giant year-round agricultural industry; the need to create a transportation infrastructure to facilitate delivery of products to and from the Southwest and West; and, most important, the shortages of available labor that occurred during World War I.

Although taking on many spontaneous and individualistic characteristics, this massive migration was at first

105

planned in many aspects, but in the long run it spawned independent patterns of migration characteristic today:

> A new phase of the labor history of Hispanics in the United States began around the turn of the twentieth century, when employers in the Southwest, and soon afterward the Midwest, began to recruit workers from the Mexican border. Their efforts set in motion a movement that has shaped migration patterns from Mexico throughout the twentieth century. Using labor contractors and other recruiters, they brought in workers from Mexico to perform largely unskilled, low-paying tasks. This planned labor migration quickly stimulated another pattern of individual migration that took on an independent character of its own and outpaced the rate of migration by labor recruitment. (Valdez, 326)

It is estimated that some 250,000 Mexicans immigrated to the United States legally.[39] Between 1920 and 1929, some 500,000 additional Mexicans immigrated to the United States. (Briggs, 142–143) Although there was significant representation of Mexicans from the educated, professional, and entrepreneurial classes who emigrated mostly as political and/or religious refugees—and they were very important in creating central institutions in the Mexican-American communities—the overwhelming representation of working-class Mexicans necessarily created a generalized image in the United States of Mexicans as uneducated, unskilled workers. But more specifically, American entrepreneurs responsible for importing Mexican labor to the United States valued Mexicans because they were supposedly docile and easily manipulated. They believed that most Mexican immigrants were Indian peons, whose low intelligence, lack of ambition, and acceptance of low wages were their most attractive attributes. (Reisler, 25) In fact, it was their supposed indolence and sloth that justified their substandard wages. One

Texas cotton grower testified to Congress in 1920 that "there never was a more docile animal in the world than the Mexican." (Senate Committee on Immigration, 4) In addition, Mexicans were thought to be childlike, lazy, unprogressive, and lacking moral fiber, among other stereotypes that Anglos related to race or cultural traits. (Reisler, 26–28)

The whole tradition of racializing Hispanics in the United States was now supported with scientific and pseudo-scientific studies. University professors as well as politicians began issuing reports demonstrating that Mexicans were an inferior race made up mostly of Native American stock. "More Indians have crossed the southern border in one year than lived in the entire territory of New England at the time of the Plymouth settlement. This movement is the greatest Indian migration of all time," stated Glenn Hoover in 1929. "[Immigration] Restrictionists had been able to use to good advantage the pervasive stereotype of Mexican as Indian peon. They continually stressed a dual theme: the Mexican's Indian blood would pollute the nation's genetic purity, and his biologically degenerate character traits would sap the country's moral fiber and corrupt its institutions." (Reisler, 37–38) Thus, the Mexican also bore the burden of Anglo-American attitudes toward Indians. But the farmers, in arguing against imposing restrictions on Mexican immigration said that, since European and Asian restrictions had been created, the only alternative to Mexican labor was black, Filipino, and Puerto Rican, who were worse threats to the racial purity of the United States and, most important of all, could not be deported when labor demand diminished— they were not legally aliens. (Reisler, 37)

Despite attacks from nativists, racists, and even organized labor in the United States, Mexican immigrant labor was successful in developing working-class culture as a

Border Patrol. Courtesy Harry Ransom Center, The University of Texas at Austin.

positive value and even in advancing the cause of organized labor in the United States, especially in the agricultural industries. Mexican workers, as well as other Hispanic workers, of course suffered problems endemic to people who are marginalized by lack of education and skills, undefined or limited civil rights, and lack of language skills in a foreign environment. These obstacles included exploitation, segregation, high unemployment, high crime rate, low life expectancy, etc. All of these problems, in addition to racialization, became associated with the Mexican and Hispanic image in the United States and further eroded the prestige of the Spanish language and Hispanic culture, with both becoming associated with poverty. By the 1960s theirs would be called the "culture of poverty."

In times of recession and depression, Mexican laborers became dispensable to employers throughout; significant expulsions took place in 1921–1922, during the Great Depression, in 1954, and during the 1980s. In times of economic stress, the Mexicans' low prestige jobs and low wages suddenly became attractive to other workers. Mexicans were blamed for taking "American" jobs and for bloating the

welfare rolls. During these times of stress, again, anti-Mexi-
can and anti-Hispanic prejudices ran high. The solution that
took hold was deportation; this was also a solution used by
employers to bust unionizing activities, with the assistance
of the Immigration and Naturalization Service (INS). During
the Great Depression, the United States effected the largest
mass deportations of an ethnic group in its history. Between
1931 and 1939, federal and local authorities "repatriated"
more than four hundred thousand people to Mexico, including Mexican Americans who had been born in the United
States. (Hoffman, chapter 4)

Some of the humiliation and agony of the Repatriation
are documented in the famous folk ballad from the 1930s,
"El Corrido del Deportado" (The Ballad of the Deportee):

Los güeros son muy maloras,
los güeros son muy maloras,
se valen de la ocasión.

Y a todos los mexicanos,
y a todos los mexicanos,
nos tratan sin compasión.

Ahí traen la gran polvadera,
ahí traen la gran polvadera,
y sin consideración.

Mujeres, niños y ancianos
los llevan a la frontera,
nos echan de esta nación.

Adiós, paisanos queridos,
adiós, paisanos queridos,
ya nos van a deportar.

Pero no somos bandidos,
pero no somos bandidos,
venimos a camellar.

[The white people are bad news,
the white people are bad news,
they take advantage of the opportunity.

And to all us Mexicans,
and to all us Mexicans,
they treat us without compassion.

Look at the large cloud of dust,
look at the large cloud of dust,
they don't even care.

Women, children and aged
they are driving to the border.
They're throwing us out of this nation.

Goodbye, my dear countrymen,
goodbye, my dear countrymen,
they're about to deport us.

But we're not bandits,
but we're not bandits,
we came to work like beasts.]

Aside from comprehending the vulnerability and flexibility of the Mexican labor pools in the United States, employers had learned that they could treat the flow of Mexican and other Hispanic labor (notably Puerto Rican and other Hispanic Caribbean workers) as water in a spigot that could be turned on and off with the ebb and flow of economic cycles. Thus, while European immigration, even of Jewish refugees (until the 1948 Displaced Persons Act), had been shut off during World War II, the U.S. and the Mexican governments created the first of a series of temporary worker programs to funnel Mexican labor initially to the agricultural fields and the railroads and later into other nonskilled labor. Both governments considered the creation of the program an important part of the war effort. The Mexican government, however, was at first resistant to the new efforts to contract its laborers because of the recent abuses and deportations of Mexicans. Thus, the Mexican government insisted that the agreement, worked out in 1942, include guaranteed minimum wages, worker protection, and an organized system for workers to return to Mexico once their contracts were up.

The Mexican Labor Agreement, sanctioned by Congress in 1943 as Public Law 45, but popularly known as the Bracero Program, went through various metamorphoses and expansions. The program was finally terminated in 1964, largely through the efforts of unions and Mexican Americans who suffered depressed wages and opportunities as a result of the program, and who also demonstrated that the Mexican contract laborers were being mistreated, as usual. The termination of the program helped pave the way for the successful unionizing efforts in agriculture that took place during the late 1960s and the 1970s.

Braceros *leaving Mexico City for the United States. Courtesy Arte Público Press. Photo by Hermanos Mayo.*

At its peak in the late 1950s, the Bracero Program contracted more than four hundred thousand workers seasonally. (Valdez, 336) According to U.S. statistics, a total of 4,591,538 laborers were contracted through the Bracero Program. (García y Greigo,

Migrant labor housing.
Courtesy Library of Congress.

77) Many other workers not in the program were drawn to the United States at the same time, thus bloating the worker pool and further depressing unionizing activities and the availability of work for legal residents and American citizens, including Mexican Americans. In fact, the unauthorized migration of labor that took place outside of the Bracero Program became so large that the U.S. government, in order to regularize the labor flow, began officially recognizing the unauthorized or undocumented migrants as *braceros*. During the years 1947 to 1949 only 74,600 laborers were imported from Mexico while 142,000 deportable Mexicans already here were legalized and put under contract. The number of undocumented workers continued to grow, with 96,239 put under contract and only 19,813 imported in 1951. (García y Griego, 57) In order to regain control, the INS embarked on a massive, military-style campaign to round up and deport undocumented Mexican labor. Supported by the government and public opinion, which blamed "wetbacks" for labor unrest, spreading diseases, communist infiltration, crime, and union-busting, Operation

Wetback was responsible for the deportation of more than one million undocumented workers.

In all, the Bracero Program established patterns of labor immigration, both formal and informal, that would continue to the present. It encompassed all of the dynamics that would characterize migration henceforth: legal, regularized migration and undocumented flow both formally and informally sanctioned by industry and government, as well as an ostentatious program of deportations while allowing industry to continue to depend on undocumented workers. As García y Griego summarizes,

Woman farm worker during World War II. Courtesy Library of Congress.

> The migration of workers stimulated and regulated by the contract-labor program is not an aberration in the history of Mexican immigration to the United States. ... The bracero migration not only continued the labor migration of the earlier period, it reaffirmed the notion that the northward movement of Mexicans is a single process. Braceros and undocumented (and, to a limited

Migrant labor camp. Courtesy Library of Congress.

113

extent, legally admitted) immigrants were substituted for each other. After 1954, the "success" of Operation Wetback signified the substitution of braceros for "wetbacks"—at labor standards substantially below those afforded by contract-labor guarantees. After 1964, some braceros were replaced by "wetbacks" and others by machines; the elite within the bracero labor force immigrated legally and became the permanent residents or

Cotton picker.
Courtesy Library of Congress.

"green card commuters." Thus, throughout the contract labor period and since then, the formal conditions of Mexican labor migration—i.e., the labels assigned to it—varied from time to time, but the informal patterns of migration persisted. (71)

The labor demands of World War II also stimulated the largest wave of Puerto Rican migration to the United States. Puerto Ricans had been incorporated into the U.S. labor pool since the Spanish American War, and outmigration to the Northeastern Seaboard was produced as small farmers became dislocated from their lands when U.S. corporations gained control of the best agricultural properties. By 1930, three-fifths of the sugar production in Puerto Rico was controlled by just four U.S. corporations, which were responsible for more than two-thirds of employment on the island. (Valdez, 327) During World War I, the newly baptized U.S. citizens began moving into factory work and service industries in New York and environs. In particular, the rise and fall in the history of the coffee and sugar industries, along

114

with the modernization of the sugar industry through the introduction of machinery, created widespread unemployment in Puerto Rico that was looked upon from the outset by the colonial government as a surplus working class that should be encouraged to emigrate.[40] From that point on, emigration and migration became a way of life for Puerto Ricans. (Korrol, 284–285)

The sorrow at being forced to uproot in order to make a living elsewhere is memorialized in the following Puerto Rican folk song about migration:

> *¡Pobrecitos, pobrecitos!*
> *Miradlos como se van,*
> *Porque en su tierra se mueren.*
> *Porque en su tierra no hay pan.*
>
> *[Poor souls, poor souls!*
> *Look how they go,*
> *Because in their homeland they die.*
> *Because in their land there's no bread.]*

Between 1920 and 1930, an estimated fifty-three thousand Puerto Ricans lived in the United States and its territories, with some 80 percent of them living in New York. (Korrol, 286) Each shift in the U.S. or the Island economy registered corresponding increases in the outmigration or return migration, beginning with the thirteen thousand laborers contracted during World War I. Also, U.S. citizenship under the Jones Act of 1917 meant that Puerto Ricans could be drafted. Some eighty-three thousand served in the armed services during World Wars I and II. (Korrol, 286) The military experience was an additional stimulus for emigration.

But the floodgates opened during and after World War II when the first mass migration of workers by air was arranged by the government and employing industries. Between 1940 and 1950, the population of Puerto Ricans residing in the states rose from 69,967 to 301,375. (Korrol, 290) During the next twenty years that stateside population would grow to 1,429,664. (Rodríguez-Fraticelli, 35–47)

In 1944, the Puerto Rican government and the U.S. federal government created Operation Bootstrap to develop the island economy through the relocation of American industries to the island. The purpose was to create tax incentives, provide access to a cheap labor market, and foster policies to promote emigration to alleviate what was perceived to be the overriding problem of overpopulation. Both urban and seasonal agricultural work on the Eastern Seaboard from Florida to New England were arranged for by the Puerto Rican Department of Labor. During its peak, a net migration of some one hundred thousand workers came to the United States yearly, and counting the Puerto Ricans born in the states, eventually one-third of Puerto Ricans resided there permanently. Like the Mexicans, they, too, earned a living predominantly from factory, service, and agricultural work and helped to enlarge the ranks of working-class Hispanics and increase their exposure to exploitation and racism. In the case of the Puerto Ricans—as well as Dominicans and working-class Cubans—the racial stigma was more intense because of the greater presence of African heritage. Another folk song, "La Discriminción" (Discrimination), registers the resistance, in fact, of Puerto Ricans of African heritage to emigrate to the United States because of racism:

> *Dicen que los americanos*
> *no quieren na' de color.*
> *Aquí yo me quedo, paisanos,*
> *con mis hermanos del corazón.*

> *[They say the Americans*
> *don't want anything of color.*

116

*I'm staying here, countrymen,
with my brothers of the soul.]*

Although, as stated earlier, people of Cuban birth have always resided in what came to be the United States, and Cuban immigration was significant during the nineteenth century, large-scale Cuban immigration did not take place until the 1960s when hundreds of thousands of Cubans left the island as political refugees. The nature of Cuban immigration changed Hispanic immigration patterns dramatically as well as the development of Hispanic culture in the United States; both changes resulted in an altered Hispanic image in this country. All class sectors of Cuban society were represented in the refugee populations, but the greatest and strongest representation was of middle-class Cubans. As compared to the other ethnic working-class Hispanic immigrants, Cubans were the first large group of Hispanic immigrants prepared to prosper not in agriculture and the service industries but as professionals and entrepreneurs. With their education and business acumen, they have transformed Miami, where their largest community exists, into a dynamic center of international trade:

> Cubans in Miami created a strongly integrated, ethnically enclosed economy that provided considerable opportunities for exiles during the 1960's and 1980's. Many of the Cubans of the first exile wave in the early 1960's brought with the education, values and skills necessary to take advantage of the North American economic system. Moreover, many of them brought the required capital or gained access to it through federal and private business loans in the United States. Cubans translated these opportunities into a diverse set of economic enterprises that expanded rapidly enough to provide employment for subsequent exile waves. (Poyo and Díaz-Miranda, 307)

117

By 1980, Cubans owned more than eighteen thousand businesses in Miami's Dade County. In their population were some 3,500 doctors, 25,000 garment workers, more than 500 lawyers, 16 Cuban presidents of banks, and 250 bank vice presidents. Cubans owned more than 60 new and used car dealerships, 500 supermarkets, and 250 drug stores. (Poyo and Díaz-Miranda, 307) Although the median family income of Cubans has not reached the level of Anglo-Americans, they do surpass that of other Hispanic ethnic groups. (Pérez, 1–20) But educational and economic background alone do not fully explain the Cuban success story. According to Poyo and Miranda,

> This economic success resulted from a variety of factors, including the demographic characteristics of migratory flows, the active support of the Cubans by the United States government as a result of their refugee status, the benefits of Miami's enclave economy and the success of Cuban women in entering the labor market and contributing substantially to family incomes. (309)

As in the cases of U.S. historical involvement and intervention in Latin American countries such as Haiti, Nicaragua, and Santo Domingo, the American support of dictatorial regimes in Cuba helped to establish the United States as a destination for political refugees once the dictator in question, Fulgencio Batista, had fallen to rebel forces. What was new was that the introduction of Communism so close to the United States, where U.S. interests had been traditionally very high, was seen not only as a repudiation of capitalism but also as an extreme military danger to the United States during the cold war—and the Cuban missile crisis almost succeeded in making it a "hot" war. From that point on, Latin American countries as close as Santo Domingo and as far away as Chile were cast into the role of a battleground where the cold war was played out, with the United States supporting at least nominally anti-Communist regimes, no matter how autocratic and corrupt they might be, and the Soviet Union, often through Cuba itself, funding insurgent nationalist movements in Latin America.

The die was cast for the United States to continue supporting military regimes in Central America and for U.S. involvement to result in emigration of displaced persons to the United States. The late 1980s thus experienced dramatic increases in immigration—it was largely disputed whether they were political or economic refugees—from El Salvador, Guatemala, and Nicaragua. Immigration policy from the 1960s to the 1980s had thus become firmly entrenched as a tool of international relations. By 1989, immigration from the Americas had risen to 61.4 percent of the total, with Mexico accounting for 37.1 percent and El Salvador 5.2 percent. (Valdez, 334) But any figures for Hispanic immigration during the postwar period may be doubled by the unaccounted for undocumented immigrants—the total figure has always remained a mystery. Legal immigration was almost as high in the 1980s as in the 1900s: legal immigration during the first decade of the century reached 8.8 million, whereas during the 1980s it reached 6.3 million, with Hispanics accounting for more than 40 percent of the 1980s total. (Valdez, 335)

Immigration from Cuba came in three waves, reflecting the ups and downs of relations between Washington, D.C., and Castro—1960–1962, 1965–1973, and 1980—and ultimately was responsible for the entry of more than one million Cubans who at first thought that their sojourn in the United States would be temporary. The flows and stoppages of migration by both parties came to be used not only as a tool in foreign relations but as a propaganda motive in the ideological confrontation of the cold war. According to

Mitchell, "Under presidential leadership the United States welcomed this large group of émigrés, intending to drain skilled workers from the Cuban revolutionary regime and simultaneously to undermine that government's prestige."[41] And Fidel Castro hoped to embarrass the United States' efforts to welcome educated, professional, middle-class Cuban refugees by opening the doors of prisons and mental institutions and facilitating a boatlift of the predominantly working class and previously institutionalized Cubans through the port of Mariel in 1980 and once again in 1994. For the first time, in 1994, an American president, Bill Clinton, stemmed the tide of Cuban refugees by returning them to Cuba and/or temporarily diverting them to Panama. With the cold war over, Russian presence in Cuba had terminated and anti-immigrant sentiment in the United States had escalated. Taking Cuban refugees in no longer had propaganda value; it furthermore would have overburdened the immigration and social services already dealing with extensive immigration from Haiti, Mexico, and Central America.

Similarly, the U.S.-backed assassination of dictator Rafael Trujillo in the Dominican Republic in 1961 was aimed at averting a Cuban-style communist revolution and led to the establishment of immigration pathways that have brought some five hundred thousand Dominicans to live in the United States. With Cuban, Mexican, and Dominican immigration at record levels, for the first time in its history Congress restricted visas for the Western Hemisphere to 120,000 per year, and in 1976 extended the preference system and the annual 20,000 annual limit per county. (Mitchell, 15–22) Of course, this led to intensified efforts by undocumented immigrants to enter the United States, a problem that had not been adequately addressed to date. The "illegal" immigrant has become a *cause celebre* for nativists and conservative politicians but has also resulted in various amnesty programs for "illegal" residents of the United States.

It was President Ronald Reagan who pursued the battle against Communism in Cuba and Central America to its fullest, and he unwittingly succeeded in precipitating the migration of hundreds of thousands of refugees from El Salvador, Nicaragua, and Guatemala to the United States as a by-product of U.S. military and/or political involvement in those countries. While the immigrants from Central America were similar to the Mexicans and Puerto Ricans in their predominantly working-class backgrounds, the example of Cuban skilled and professional workers helped to redefine U.S. immigration policy toward Latin America for the first time in history: The Immigration Act of 1990 attempted to promote the immigration of skilled workers by creating a separate preference system and allocating 120,000 visas for skilled or professional workers, plus 10,000 visas each for religious workers and investors capable of creating jobs. (Mitchell, 18) Unification of families was a high priority in the 1990 act, as it had been in previous laws. The 1990 act also permitted Salvadorans and Guatemalans fleeing violence in their homelands to remain legally in the United States as opposed to their persecution by the INS under Reagan.

While the Cuban diaspora and the U.S. government's backing of Cuban settlement and accommodation in the United States did much to diversify the image of Hispanics projected in the media, in business and as reflected in legislation there were many other factors operating during the latter part of the twentieth century that brought a more diverse Hispanic population into the national conscience. The immediate effect of Mexican American, Puerto Rican, and other Hispanics having shed their blood on foreign soil during World War II and the Korean War was the creation of a sense of entitlement among the returning veterans, who set up civil rights organizations to advance their status as American citizens and claim the rights due them. The GI Bill accounted for advances in education and housing for Hispanic veterans through low-cost loans offered to them. Their children became the first generation of Hispanics to benefit on a large scale from admission to state colleges and universities precisely at the time, during the Kennedy-Johnson years, that the Great Society had created numerous social and education programs to create access to education and work. The desegregation of education after *Brown v. Board of Education* and the Civil Rights Act of 1964, the various voting rights acts, the Bilingual Education Act, and several Supreme Court decisions desegregating the schools and protecting equal access to education ensured the movement of a larger number of Hispanics into education and the professions.

The last two decades have seen Hispanics elected to state legislatures throughout the Southwest, Florida, the Northeast, and Illinois. Major cities in the Southwest, such as Denver and San Antonio, have had Hispanics as mayors for the first time in modern history. Hispanics have been appointed to federal benches and to presidential cabinet positions. There are Hispanic astronauts, sports stars (the major sports once barred Hispanics of color), actors, popular and classical musicians, and performers. There are three Spanish-language television networks, hemispheric in their broadcasts, but all centered and administered in the United States; there are hundreds of Spanish-language radio stations, newspapers, and periodicals publishing today. Hispanics have become the essential link to the rest of the hemisphere to the south and have already pioneered this linkage on their own through media, banking, import-export, and many other endeavors that enrich the nation and create a basis for future partnerships within the Americas, such as the North

American Free Trade Agreement (NAFTA). The Hispanic population of the United States (including undocumented residents) today makes up the largest minority: more than thirty million strong, although the median age is still in the early teens and most Hispanics are in the school population. Their economic power and their burgeoning demographic power mean that they can soon vote with the ballot and the dollar.

In 1996, the U.S. Census Bureau predicted that Latinos and Asians would account for more than half of the growth in the population of the United States every year for at least fifty years. The result will be a great change in the ethnicity of the United States. By the year 2050, non-Hispanic whites will only be a bare majority. As of July 1995, the total population of the United States was 262.8 million, but is estimated to climb to 393.9 million by the year 2050. While the rate of general population growth will shrink over the next fifty years, the rate of growth of the Hispanic population will actually increase. By the year 2050, the Hispanic population is predicted to make up 24.5 percent of the total population, making Hispanics by far the largest minority group in the United States, and almost half of the size of the non-Hispanic white population. The Census Bureau expects immigration of 820,000 per year, including about 225,000 undocumented persons. The Hispanic population in 1996 was growing at a rate of 900,000 per year, including net immigration of 350,000. Even without immigration, the Hispanic population would be the fastest growing because it is younger and has a higher fertility rate. The largest growth in the Hispanic population will take place in the states of California, Texas, New York, Florida, Illinois, and New Jersey, in that order. However, there is now a spillover effect, with immigrant communities growing in such areas as Atlanta, Minneapolis, and Washington State.

Today, Hispanics still predominate in the ranks of the working class and poverty stricken, with unskilled and blue-collar workers most represented. Race, language, and lack of education still represent very high barriers to advancement toward the American Dream. Periodically, nativists, white power groups, and even other working-class and ethnic groups that fear competition from Hispanics, still move to stop immigration, declare English the only language of public discourse and entitlement, and eliminate bilingual education, affirmative action, and welfare in an effort to curb Hispanic presence and influence in the United States.

Despite all of the contributions that have been made by Hispanics toward developing the country—in working within the economic and political systems, in creating great potential for improving the U.S. business and political leadership in the hemisphere—the English-language media rarely present images of Hispanics, and when they do they are usually images of crime and poverty or the inherited stereotypes from generations past. English-language newspaper and book publishing, television, and film not only continue to resist employing Hispanics in their companies[42] but also keep them off their pages and screens when depicting the current American scene and the mythological West.[43] The western landscape as depicted in motion pictures is devoid of Mexicans, except for bandidos and background scenery; today's urban scene is devoid of Hispanics except for gang members and drug dealers. If Hispanic women are depicted, they are the sultry temptresses of low morals, Latin spitfires, or long-suffering mothers of debased children. And they all still speak a horribly broken English with a stage Spanish accent. The most powerful media in the United States continue to erase Hispanics from the landscape of American life and culture, except when they are furthering the old stereotypes. Why?

124

Chapter Five

MEDIA
IMAGES

As we have seen, many of the stereotypes of Hispanics that have persisted over the twentieth century were those that had roots in the Spanish Black Legend and Manifest Destiny. In the nineteenth century, those stereotypes were disseminated broadly by newspapers, popular literature, and entertainments as well as in the books of some of the nation's most notable and respected thinkers and creative writers. In Evans's review of nineteenth-century newspapers in Texas and California, he identified hundreds of articles that denigrated the Mexican and Hispanic inhabitants of the Southwest in order to justify settlement and exploitation by the recently arrived Anglo-Americans and further the doctrine of Manifest Destiny. He further traced the development of the stereotype of the Mexican bandit in these newspapers.[44] Numerous other studies have adequately documented the century and a half of yellow journalism practices against Hispanics as well as the stereotyping, scapegoating, and unduly associating Hispanics with crime, as in southern California newspapers' persecution of "zoot-suiters" during and after World War II.[45] From the post–World War II period on, we are of course familiar with how representation of

Hispanics in the news media, television, and film entertainment is more often than not as criminals.

But it was in the world of nineteenth- and early twentieth-century fiction that the stereotypes became most pervasive and had the longest-lasting impact. In conquest fiction—that body of literature memorializing the conquest of the West, rather than agonizing over the morality of expropriating the lands of other nations—the most celebrated writers supported the expansion south by west with graphic descriptions of the inferior peoples encountered and conquered by the racially robust Euro-Americans that came to be known as Anglo-Americans.

> That few writers saw anything unconscionable about the conquest means that in fiction, at least, the long-term moral burden of the conflict has proven to be a very light one. Literary agonizing over the trauma of black slavery or the taking of a continent from the Indians in the nineteenth century has not echoed in fictional treatments of the annexation of the vast south-western territories from the Mexicans in the same century. (Pettit, 1980, 18)

Clearly, the first battleground in the war between the forces of the divinely chosen "Saxon" conquerors and the dark-skinned "foreigners" was the war of secession of Texas from Mexico. Such writers as Anthony Ganilh and Jeremiah Clemens, and a host of others, not only promoted the superiority of the Anglos but insisted that Texas should conquer the rest of Mexico. (Pettit, 1980, 22) Pettit has explained how the racial and political climate in the United States was reflected in the fictive depiction of a racially superior Anglo-Saxon over an inferior dark-skinned Mexican during and after the Texas Revolution:

> The "Tex-Mex" as a formula scoundrel in these early novels is the victim of three forces beyond his control:

the fictional need for villains who offer maximum contrast to the heroes; the actual presence of some difference in skin color between the two ethnic groups; and the unabashed racial bigotry that characterized the United States between the first years of manifest destiny and the outbreak of the Civil War. In an era preoccupied by fear of abolition and "miscegenation" and bombarded with pamphlets and lectures by quack ethnologists, abolitionists, and slave owners, it is not surprising that a good many authors who chose as a theme the Texas Revolution—many of them native southerners— easily transferred long-established notions about one dark-skinned race to another. A consistent central theme of these novels is that the "pure" racial stock of the Spanish conquerors has been polluted beyond cleansing by mixing with the native populations, and that this pollution in turn largely explains the chronic cowardice of the Spaniards' contaminated offspring, the Mexicans. (Pettit, 23)

The most popular creator of these stereotypical images in his "conquest" fiction was Ned Buntline (1821–1886), who published a series of stories in the 1840s and 1850s that heavily influenced the development of Hispanic stereotypes in later "serious" fiction, but most importantly in the dime novel. Buntline consistently portrayed pure and highly principled Protestants prevailing over "arrogant hidalgos, lazy peons, evil bandidos, sexy señoritas and loose-principled priests" and is credited by Pettit with transferring the characteristic of the shuffling Sambo stereotype, with his stage dialect and comical cowardice, to the peon servants, thus creating the Hispanic buffoon type that has been with us since. Buntline also perfected the fictional depiction of the mestizo bandido with his "Spanish" intelligence and "Indian" savagery, the creation of a formula villain that would endure over a century of elaboration. (Pettit, 26–29) From

Buntline on, the only options for the Hispanic male in popular fiction were those of the bandido or buffoon. Fixed by
Buntline's time, also, was the high-born Castilian "dark lady,"
representing the old landed gentry of California and the racially "pure" European past of the Spaniard; she could win
the Jacksonian Saxon in marriage as he rescued her family
ranch or hacienda from the ruin of her inept father and/or
brother. Competing with the blonde heroines in these novels was also the half-breed Mexican harlot, who was particularly seductive to Victorian readers; she could bed the
heroes but never marry them. Clearly, she is the anteced-
ent of the sensuous Latin spitfire of Hollywood talkies.

Among the most canonized American writers to continue
these stereotypes in their serious works were such authors as
Stephen Crane and O. Henry. In "Horses—One Dash," for instance, Crane depicts the Mexican buffoon servant as a side-
kick to a Texas Ranger who puts a cringing bandido in his place.
Whereas this type of tale was rare in Crane, O. Henry created
a whole series of Heart of the West tales that almost system-
atically denigrated Mexicans, who were pictured as filthy
bandidos attempting to assault Saxon damsels invariably rescued by blonde or red-headed supermen. In "An Afternoon
Miracle," the hero Buckley beats the bandit Leandro García,
barehanded against his knife with "the good old Saxon knock-
out blow—always so pathetically disastrous to the fistless Latin
races." (O. Henry, 261) Typical of the stage dialect of O. Henry's
bandidos is that displayed in the same story, as García attempts
to assault the damsel:

> "I no hurt-y you, Senorita. ... But maybeso take one
> *beso*—one li'l kees, you call him. ..."
> "Vamoose, quick," she ordered peremptorily, "you
> coon!" The red insult burned through the Mexican's
> dark skin.

"Hidalgo, Yo!" he shot between his fangs. "I am not neg-r-ro! *Diabla bonita,* for that you shall pay me." (O. Henry, 261)

In O. Henry and Crane as well, the trend began of using Mexicans as part of the local color of the Southwest. In dime novels, for instance, the Mexican bandit was often integral to the plot and a somewhat worthy adversary for the hero, whereas in writers like Crane and O. Henry, slapstick "greasers" were harmless, just functioning as servants running errands, hanging around alleys, and sleeping in haylofts. In effect, the Mexicans of the Southwest were fading into the background consciousness in fiction as they were in real life through segregation and the overwhelming growth of the Anglo population. Even today in many novels and films set in the Southwest, Hispanics are in the background, blending into the scenery with the cacti. Of course, the western formula novel, as practiced by Zane Grey and Max Brand, continued to repeat the aforementioned stereotypes, but their most recurrent rendition of Mexican-American culture was in the person of the buffoon bandits. Posing very little threat to hero and heroine, they usually bungled the capture of the heroine or the showdown with the hero. Grey specialized in "little swarthy-skinned greaser runts" who just come close to debauching the heroines. (Pettit, 117) Again, this stereotype has continued to the present in fiction. And, Grey and Brand were particularly important in this evolution because so many of their stories made the transition into film and television.

It was not the full-length novels of more serious writers, however, that fixed these stereotypes in the mass mind, but the dime novels of no more than 30,000 words that were produced as in a deluge and sold on newsstands throughout the country. Their impact was further heightened by

129

their stories being coupled with the illustrations of engravers and cartoonists who recognized practically no limits in graphically defaming entire peoples or "races," to use their term. The publishing houses competed intensely to serve this first truly mass audience in U.S. history by escalating the level of violence and bloodshed, the depravity of the villains, and the purity of the heroes and heroines. The books always exploited shock value and sensationalism in this first planting and fashioning of the epic of the West centrally in the consciousness of American identity.

The Beadle & Adams Publishing House was the largest publisher of dime novels and featured "half-breed" bandidos in roughly one-fifth of its novels. These bandidos were characterized by features and traits that still characterize the Hispanic criminal stereotype: long greasy hair, scraggly mustaches, grotesque dialect, dark complexions, and cowardly behavior. (Pettit, 39–40) But the overall indicator of the level of evil and cowardice of the Hispanic characters in these novels and, most especially of the bandido, was skin color:

> Whether contemporary tales of the Texas Revolution, dime novels and weekly pulps, or historical romances after the pattern of Margaret Mitchell, such fiction emphasizes color as an ultimate determinate of character. "Good" or "upper-crust" Mexicans are invariably light. Color determines whether Mexican women will be cast-off harlots or first-lead Castilian heroines who might qualify as mates for the Saxon heroes. Color determines whether Mexican men are to be foes or friends. (Pettit, 57–58)

In the early twentieth century, the Buffalo Bill Stories surpassed the Beadle series in popularity and sales, and also surpassed it in the number of stereotypical Mexican characters it included in its pages: some two hundred out of a total of six hundred novels in the series included Mexican characters. (Pettit, 43) In the years that followed, numerous other houses published the dime novels and continued to spread the negative Hispanic images. Most noteworthy of all was the Wild West Weekly Series, issued by Frank Toussey Publishers in New York, issuing some 1,294 episodes from 1902 to 1928. In the publications that followed Beadle & Adams', increasingly the Anglo heroes represented authority in the form of U.S. marshals or Texas Rangers. Thus, the Mexican male in the form of bandido was pitted against the whole society, not just a robust, blonde Saxon hero.

The entry of these stereotypes into entertainment media, most notably motion pictures, can be traced to the immense popularity of the dime novel at the end of the nineteenth century. Pettit and other media historians agree that the dime novel was the most direct source for the depiction of Hispanic stereotypes in the motion picture industry at the time of its inception.[46] Those stereotypes were fixed and continued in motion pictures to this day. And Pettit, after studying hundreds of Western dime novels and novels from the nineteenth and twentieth centuries, and their filmic renditions, concurs with this book's thesis about the pervasiveness of the coherently negative image of Hispanics as shaped by the doctrine of Manifest Destiny:

> When the [Anglo-American] set out to bring democracy, progress, and Protestantism to the Hispanic Southwest, he could find a place for the Mexican in what he soon regarded as "his" Southwest only if the Mexican would become, insofar as his limited talents permitted, what the American perceived himself to be: enterprising, steady, and Protestant—in a word, civilized. Yet, somehow the Mexican remained something else in the Anglo-American's eye: shiftless, unreliable, and alternately decadent or barbaric. Thus, it seemed the American's

131

manifest destiny to conquer and convert this errant
race. In the process it was also necessary to destroy a
culture the Mexican would not willingly surrender.
Operating from such moral absolutes, the Anglo was
able to achieve a satisfactory interpretation of his racial
and cultural superiority. He could flatter himself that he
was not deprecating a race but standing up for civilization. He could persuade himself, in fact, that he was not
guilty of racism in any sense that we understand the
term. For if the Mexican could only be evaluated in
terms of the civilization to which, by the laws of nature,
God, and history alike, he had to give way, then how
could the conqueror be blamed for what was destined
to happen? The Anglo-American thus came to see the
indigenous way of life in what became the American
Southwest as inherently and irrevocably inferior and
hostile to his own institutions. (Pettit, xvii–xviii)

The most repeated of these stereotypes in film was the
dirty, unkempt, cowardly bandido who wore a large sombrero and crossed bandoleros whose real-life roots lay in
the social rebels like Joaquín Murieta and Mexican revolutionaries like Pancho Villa, both of whom, it must be noted,
had caused great fear among Anglos. The Hispanic villain,
often a bandido, has been a constant, beginning with some of
the first films of the silent cinema, including "greaser" films
such as *Bronco Billy and the Greaser* (1914) and D. W. Griffith's
epics, in which the famed director standardized and passed
on a style of racial stereotyping that is still current in motion
pictures today, as in such gang movies as *West Side Story*
(1961), *Fort Apache the Bronx* (1981), and *Colors* (1988), and
such television crime shows as *Hill Street Blues, Starsky and
Hutch, Kojac, Miami Vice,* and numerous others. The
bandido's counterpart was a half-breed harlot, with her low-
cut blouse, rose behind her ear, her hot temper, and her
sexual promiscuity.

By the advent of the 1930s, films personified the sexual attractiveness and passion of the Hispanic—probably threatening to the more reserved Anglo culture—in the ubiquitous Latin lover and the dark lady, the former a mixture of sensuality and exotic sexual danger, the latter mysterious, virginal, aristocratic. Whereas the dark lady started out as a brooding, vengeful and dangerous wench, actress Lupe Vélez in the 1930s and 1940s elevated the stereotype to stardom by making her volatile and verbal, exhibiting overt sexuality, a hot temper, and mood shifts, spewing broken English full of malapropisms and comic misunderstandings. Thus, a new stereotype was born that eventually made it into television days: the Latin spitfire.

The "Dark Lady," María Montez.
Courtesy Library of Congress.

In addition to these stereotypes, a variety of male and female buffoons also survived the transition to motion pictures. During the 1930s as well the bandido began to undergo a transformation into the greaser gangster, who "differed from the Anglo model established by such stars as James Cagney and George Raft. He is a coward. He invariably is treacherous ... oily and ugly, crude and overdressed, in no way a romantic figure even when considered as a man outside society." (Pettit, 143) In the postwar period, the bandido and greaser gangster were reincarnated into the street gang leader and the drug trafficker. All of these stereotypes still have currency on television and in film. (Subervi, 308–310) From bandido to Latin lover and spitfire, in film and television, the Hispanic "remains a subject—someone to be killed, mocked, seduced or redeemed by Saxon protagonists." (Pettit, 132) Pettit goes on to further characterize the depiction of Mexicans, in particular, in the early cinema:

Famed "Latin Lover" Ricardo Montalbán. Courtesy Library of Congress.

> The mass of Mexican characters in the early cinema seems to support the assumption that most members of their race are evil or promiscuous, cowardly or inept. Given these fixed racial traits, it seems axiomatic that individual or collaborative repentance and atonement for all Mexican "crimes" and "sins" committed against

American heroes and heroines is simply out of the
question. Whether as villains or buffoons, halfbreed
sluts or "white" dark ladies, celluloid Mexicans tend to
be treated as a series of shadow figures: cutouts and
puppets whose behavior is as wooden as it is uncon-
vincing. By the end of the first half-century of Hollywood cinema, the artistic image of the Mexican was still
one of the gullible greaser, capable at best of a primitive
and unreliable allegiance to white folks—and for that
reason more to be ridiculed and reviled than admired,
respected, or even feared. (Pettit, 150–151)

The development of the Hollywood Formula of commu-
nicating Americanism and providing wish fulfillment was
particularly harmful to minorities, as Keller points out:

In American film, the ethnic *other* strictly and almost
invariably played the outcast or evildoer. Film, and for
that matter, television in its early period, was an instru-
ment of socialization that took as its guiding premise
the assimilation of all racial, ethnic, and religious
differences into the harmonizing credo of the American
melting pot. There was no room whatsoever for diver-
gence from this requirement. Even more painful, those
races and ethnicities that could not be readily assimi-
lated because of their differences of color and physiog-
nomy—which would be readily apparent on the
black-and white-celluloid—for example, blacks, Hispanics, and Indians, were drummed into the fold of evildo-
ers and outcasts, a priori and without recourse. Blacks,
Hispanics and Indians consequently functioned as the
slag of the melting-pot alchemy of American film.
(Keller, 549)

In the face of constant denigration of its people and government on Hollywood screens, Mexico vigorously protested
both to the U.S. government and to the film industry numerous times throughout this century. In 1919, the Mexican

government put Hollywood on call through a letter to film producers, protesting their emphasis on "films of squalor" in which "photographers travel about, seeking the worst conditions they can find, and compose their films entirely of such pictures." (Woll, 17) The letter ended with a threat of restricting filming on location in Mexico, but of course the warning was not heeded. In 1922, the Mexican government took the step of banning all films that portrayed Mexicans unfavorably, and to intensify the policy later banned *all films* by the company that produced the defamatory one. A government official explained that "the usual portrayal of the Mexican in moving pictures is as a bandit or a sneak. Ill will toward Mexico has been inflamed by these pictures to such an extent that the Mexican government found it necessary to make such a protest."[47] According to Woll,

> This was quite a strong ultimatum to be delivered at the height of the American film industry's expansion southward. The Famous Players-Lasky offices, which had just completed a one-hundred-film deal with Mexican distributors, was shaken by the pronouncement and issued a statement saying that "the wishes of the government would be respected." (17–18)

The Mexican action was followed by Panama, which went even further in not only banning denigrating films "tending to discredit or lower the prestige of the country" but also levied fines on anyone who produced photographs that "discredit the race or misrepresent national customs."[48] Hollywood's response was not to alter stereotypes but to switch locales to areas farther south: to Argentina and Brazil. Thus, a spate of late-1920s films began featuring Latin lovers and dark ladies in Buenos Aires and Rio de Janeiro in such forgettable B-films as *Argentine Love* (1924) and *The Gaucho* (1927). In 1930, the Chilean ambassador protested to none less than Secretary of

Commerce of the United States Herbert Hoover while at a dinner for motion picture advertisers:

> The myth of Spanish-American lovers serenading their fair ladies under iron-grilled balconies bathed by romantic moonlight and alive with the beauty of red carnations; and the injustice of portraying all those who hail from south of the Rio Grande as born villains to be conquered by the mighty, iron-fisted, two-gunned vigilante; and the perpetuation of such absurdities as picturing an Argentine gentleman on his wedding day in the brilliant dress of a bullfighter, when the colorful Spanish entertainment is forbidden in that progressive country—these are things that we call, with a friendly smile of forbearance, *Hollywoodisms*.[49]

But traveling so far south on location was impractical, and the next solution was to set the films in mythical Latin countries, and, at least in place names, disguise the Mexican setting. Of course, these manufactured settings fooled no one, nor did the stereotyped portrayals of what otherwise would have been Mexican characters. So outlandish was the setting and stereotyping in *The Dove* (1928), which was set in "Costa Roja," supposedly located in the Mediterranean, that a *New York Times* critic commented, "Taken by and large, José is perhaps a screen character to which the Mexican government might have objected, for he is greedy, sensuous, boastful, cold-blooded, irritable, and quite a wine bibber. ..."[50]

When *The Dove* was remade in the sound era as *The Girl of the Rio* (1932), Leo Carrillo, the son of an old Californio family, portrays one of the vilest greaser gangsters in film history: Señor Tostado (Mr. Toast—an obvious reference to skin color). Tostado is interested only in money, drink, sex, and violence. Carrillo pursues an Anglo beauty in love with Johnny Powell, who Tostado frames for murder in order to force the girl to go off with him. The producers set it in a

137

Mexican bordertown, and once again Mexico issued a threat to ban all of the products of motion pictures that produced films denigrating Mexican people or the Mexican nation. (Woll, 21) Mexico was not alone in the sound era in issuing protests and banning films. As Woll states, "All of Latin America was still being depicted as a cultural backwater, populated by evil bandits and dancing maidens." (32) In 1931, the Brazilian government requested that the U.S. Department of State repress *Rio's Road to Hell* (1931) and the Cuba's Motion Picture Exhibitors' Union banned all MGM films until *Cuban Love Song* (1931) was taken off the market. In 1932, Panama and Nicaragua also banned *The Girl of the Rio*. In the years that followed, many Spanish-American countries signed treaties with each other and with Spain to ban films that defamed Hispanics and their countries.

The only real departure from these stereotypical trends and tendencies was a period during World War II when President Franklin D. Roosevelt promoted the Good Neighbor Policy in order to secure Latin American alliance and support. But Hollywood did not support Roosevelt's policy solely out of idealism or commitment to the war effort; the war in Europe cut deeply into profits of films distributed in Europe at the same time that the German film industry had greatly advanced in producing Spanish-language films for Spanish America. Thus, Latin America really became the prime market for U.S. film exports, and Hollywood needed to secure that market with movies that treated the Hispanic countries more positively.[51] Roosevelt's policy and Hollywood's growing recognition of the threatened Spanish-American export market translated into some positive depictions in film. It was an era when most of the bandits disappeared from the screen and a number of Hispanic actors and actresses rose to stardom, including César Romero,

María Montez, Dolores del Río, Ricardo Montalbán, and Fernando Lamas, although most of them still were cast as the softer stereotypes of the Latin lover and the Latin spitfire. It was also the era when Afro-Caribbean music was exposed to the masses, bringing on a boom in popular culture for the rumba and later other Latin dances, such as the mambo and the cha-cha-cha, during the immediate post-war period.

"Latin Spitfire" Carmen Miranda.
Courtesy Library of Congress.

By 1939, such an important studio as Warner Brothers was producing serious Hispanic-themed films including the biography of Mexican President Benito Juárez. However, for the most part, other than the Juárez film and another about Simón Bolívar, Hollywood's South American cycle of films was full of cultural misunderstanding and was poorly received in Spanish America. Once the war was over and European and Asian markets opened up and ballooned over the demand in Spanish America, Hollywood gradually went back to populating films with gross stereotypes of Hispanics, reaching its nadir of defamation in the gang and drug culture films of the 1970s and 1980s. But the Mexican buffoon and the Mexican bandit also lived on, a phenomenon that film historian Woll has called "the return of the greaser":

> By the mid-1960's, as violence returned to the modern screen, a new villain was resurrected. Whether in the

139

Street Gang from the film Boulevard Nights. *Courtesy Library of Congress.*

spaghetti westerns of Sergio Leone or the films of
Sam Peckinpah, the murderous, treacherous, and
violent Latin American reappeared on the screen.
With the new heights of filmic savagery presented on
the screen during the last decade, violence by Latin
bandits became excessive and widespread. Whereas
during the silent era the greaser might vent his wrath
on individuals or small groups, modern screen technology allows the Mexican to destroy mass portions
of the population. ...

The films of the modern era have thus reinstated
myths about the Latin American which had remained
dormant for fifteen years. At this writing [1977], a new
set of rules governing portrayals of Latin Americans
seems to be in effect: 1) The Latin American is extraordi-
narily violent. 2) The Latin American, whether peasant,
landlord, revolutionary, or whatever, is the subject of
scorn or ridicule. 3) Yet, no matter how violent the Latin
American, he is unable to cope with either the strength
or superior technology of the North American hero.
(106–108)

140

The Good Neighbor period and the Latin dance craze also intensified the stereotype of Latin sensuality, as supposedly evidenced in Latin dances that became a craze in the post-war period, and partially account for the initial success of the most famous television show featuring Hispanic culture: *I Love Lucy*. The show featured costar Desi Arnaz, who personified the Hispanic buffoon/Latin lover, and his off-and-on camera wife, Lucille Ball, the red-headed Anglo beauty who entertained audiences with her frantic comic routines. A very substantial part of the enchantment of this, the longest-lasting television sitcom, was the tension and titillation it provided mainstream audiences with the taboo pairing of a Latin—a Cuban who played a conga and sang Afro-Caribbean music—with an Anglo goddess in a domestic, albeit comic, drama. After all, the bedroom was just off camera to the left of the living room where most of the sitcom was set, and as Pérez Firmat has pointed out, both the show's title and its heart logo underscored the romantic/sexual relationship of two characters from different backgrounds who loved each other precisely because of their different ethnicities, even their different racial make-up—something quite revolutionary for the 1950s although not immediately obvious to viewers.[52] The show actually created a formula for an undercurrent in American life: sexual attraction for the Other. (Of course, the sexual relations were always off camera and intuited by the audience, and they were sanitized through marriage.) And the formula has continued in sitcoms to the present with the pairing of numerous WASP and ethnic characters, including a Jewish nanny, an Italian boxer cum housekeeper, a Central American maid, and others, as a metaphor for ethnic relations in the United States.

Today, more realistic and diverse images of Hispanics are beginning to be included on the silver screen and TV, with directors such as Luis Valdez and Gregory Nava creating box-office successes and actors like Andy García and Rita Moreno attracting respectable followings. In the age of affirmative action and the growth of Hispanic demographics—along with the substantial competition offered by Spanish-language television—both broadcast and cable television feature Hispanics such as Geraldo Rivera as talk show hosts and Hispanic actors such as Jimmy Smits in leading roles, even in non-Hispanic roles in crime dramas. But the overall impact of Hispanics on the large or the small screen is none at all. Where gross stereotypes and negative images have abated somewhat, the primary problem is that Hispanics are rarely depicted in English-language film and television drama and comedy; they have once again disappeared from the landscape. The one place that they are ubiquitous is in crime reports on the news, in sensationalist stories quite often read or voiced-over by Hispanic news anchors and reporters who are more "window dressing" than any real commitment to integrating the Hispanic community into media culture.

Chapter Six

CONLUSION ❖ ❖

WE ARE ON THE THRESHOLD OF A NEW CENTURY. Along with myriad other changes, the new century will see Hispanics as the largest ethnic minority in the country. Along with that status will come greater pressure for their representation in all fields of endeavor as citizens and residents of the United States. The economic, political, and even legal barriers that have denied access to Hispanics in the past are gradually crumbling. To be sure, for long into the next century Hispanics will remain a working-class people and will continue to form the backbone of many industries that make possible the American economic miracle: agriculture, construction, manufacturing, service industries, the garment industry, and others. And Hispanics will continue to develop a working-class culture in the arts and literature; they will keep the United States focused on the common person, the democratic promise, education, and opportunity for all.

Hispanics in the United States still confront an unwanted heritage: the stereotyped images inherited from the centuries of competition between the English and the Spanish, and a century and a half of Anglo-American

143

expansion and imperialism justified by ideas of racial superiority. Hispanics do not deny, but instead celebrate their mixed blood and hybrid cultures. They also celebrate their working-class background and build upon it artistically and intellectually as they continue to build up this very nation. The Western Hemisphere, including the United States, is the meeting ground of all the varieties of humankind. The Hispanics have built their culture and identity precisely on their mixed Native American-European-African background, and that mixture can be the basis for reaching out to the other peoples of the world. To date, the United States has denied its own hybrid heritage, preferring to invoke some mythic European purity or some equally mythic process of converting non-Anglo Europeans into Americans: the melting pot.

In the smaller planet of the twenty-first century, the ability to relate to and communicate with the other cultures of the world will be essential. Today it is the U.S. Hispanic peoples that have the potential for that communication more than any other group in this society. The Hispanic is the hemispheric person, par excellence, by relating ethnically and racially to all and linguistically through the two most spoken languages. More than anything, the Hispanic is New World Man/Woman; in blood, culture, geographic distribution, worldview she/he is the New Woman, the New Man.

U.S. culture as a whole can become part of this process of universalization by opening up to the heritage and contributions of all its peoples and by shucking off its mythic Old World identity, its Aryan purity, its white superiority and supremacy. There is no alternative. No white superiority movement, no nativism, no No-Nothing Party, no white backlash against affirmative action, no English-Only

144

movement, no mass deportations can turn back the clock, replace the pages of the calendar, pervert the ultimate meaning of the Declaration of Independence, the Constitution, the Bill of Rights, and the democratic processes that safeguard and make real the ideal of *e pluribus unum*.

Notes

1. The first history of one of the Spanish colonies in what would become the United States was written in 1779: Franciscan missionary Juan Agustín Morfi's *History of Texas, 1673–1779,* which documented the life of the missions, villages, and presidios during his service there. See John H. Jenkins *Basic Texas Books,* p. 387. According to the Online Computer Library Center (OCLC), the first book published by an Hispanic printer/publisher in the United Sates was W. H. Dilworth's *The Complete Letter Writer, or Young Secretary's Instructor,* issued in 1793 by Benjamin Gomez in New York. Gomez issued many other books at the end of the eighteenth century, including books by Joseph Priestley and Henry Fielding as well as John Bunyan's *Pilgrim's Progress.* OCLC records also show that the first book written and published by an Hispanic in the United States was Hipólito San Joseph Giral del Pino's *A New Spanish Grammar,* published in 1795 in Philadelphia by Colerick and Hunter. The book also included an English grammar for the use of Spaniards. Again OCLC records indicate that the first printed book in the South of what would become the United States was Louisiana Governor Bayoso de Lemos's *Deseando mantener el buen orden y tranquilidad pública* (Wishing to Maintain Good Order and Public Tranquility) issued in 1798 in New Orleans. It is also the first bilingual publication in what became the United States, with Spanish and French parallel columns.

2. See Félix Gutiérrez, "Spanish Language Media in America: Background, Resources, History," *Journalism History,* 4/2 (Summer 1977): 34-41; Nicolás Kanellos, "A Socio-Historic Study of Spanish-Language Newspapers in the United States," in *Recovering the U.S. Literary Heritage,* ed. by Ramón Gutiérrez and Genaro Padilla (Houston: Arte Público Press, 1993): 107–128.

3. Rosaura Sánchez has written extensively on the missions' educational functions as well as their exploitation of Native American labor in *Telling Identities: The Californiia Testimonies* (St. Paul: University of Minnesota Press, 1996).

4. See Rosaura Sánchez, *Telling Identities* (Minneapolis: University of Minnesota Press, 1996): 50–95, for a discussion of the importance of the missions in the growth of ranching and trade.

5. See Julián Juderías, *La leyenda negra: Estudios acerca del concepto de España en el extranjero*, thirteenth edition (Madrid: Editora Nacional, 1954).

6. See Pieter Geyl, *The Revolt of the Netherlands (1555–1609)*, second edition (London: Benn, 1980).

7. Pamphlet 1230, Koninklijke Bibliothek (The Hague), cited in Powell, *Tree of Hate* (New York: Basic Books, 1971): 68.

8. See Reginald Horsman, *Race and Manifest Destiny: The Origins of American Racial Anglo-Saxonism* (Cambridge, Mass.: Harvard University Press, 1981): 1–5.

9. See Nott and Gliddon's *Types of Mankind* (Philadelphia: Lippincott, 1854).

10. See Josiah C. Nott in *The American Whig Review,* 4 (November 1847): 280.

11. See Josiah C. Nott in *The American Whig Review,* 16 (February 1854): 148.

12. For a discussion of race in nineteenth-century schoolbooks, see Ruth Miller Elson, *Guardians of Tradition: Schoolbooks of the Nineteenth Century* (Lincoln: University of Nebraska Press, 1964).

13. See *Southern Quarterly Review* (January 21, 1852): 4.

14. In *Democratic Review* (February 18, 1846): 94.

15. See Simms's letter to John P. Kennedy, April 5, 1852, in Mary C. Simms Oliphant, Alfred Taylor Odell, and T. C. Duncan Eaves, eds. *The Letters of William Gilmore Simms,* 5 volumes. (Columbia: The University of South Carolina Press, 1952): III, 174.

148

16. Quoted in John Eaton, *The Mind of the Old South* (Baton Rouge: Louisiana State University Press, 1967): 255.

17. Quoted in Edward Mcnall Burns, *The American Idea of Mission* (Westport, Conn.: Greenwood Press, 1973): 260–261.

18. Quoted in Philip L. Nicoloff, *Emerson on Race and History: An Examination of English Traits* (New York: Columbia University Press, 1961): 119–120.

19. See Ralph Waldo Emerson, *English Traits,* ed. by Howard Mumford Jones (Cambridge, Mass.: Harvard University Press, 1966): 86.

20. See *Massachusetts Quarterly Review* (September 2, 1849): 838–840.

21. In *De Bow's Review* (March 10, 1851): 331.

22. See Caroline Crane Marsh, *Life and Letters of George Perkins Marsh* (New York: n.p., 1888): 464.

23. In Houston's inaugural address, in Amelia W. Williams and Eugene C. Barker, eds. *The Writings of Sam Houston, 1813–1863,* 8 volumes. (Austin: University of Texas Press, 1938-1943): II, 526–527.

24. *Congressional Globe*, 30th Congress, first session (March 4, 1848): 429.

25. *The American Whig Review* 4 (July 4, 1846): 14.

26. See *El Clamor Público* newspaper, April 26, 1856.

27. See Juan Nepomuceno Cortina, "Proclama," at Yale University Library, New Haven, Conn.

28. Ibid.

29. See "Corrido de Joaquín Murieta," in Antonia Castañeda Shular, Tomás Ybarra-Frausto, and Jospeh Sommers, eds. *Literatura chicana: Texto y contexto* (Englewood Cliffs, N.J.: Prentice-Hall, 1972): 65–67.

30. Interview in the *Los Angeles Star*, May 16, 1874.

31. *El Labrador*, December 20, 1904.

32. *Congressional Globe*, 30th Congress, first session, appendix (July 17, 1850): 48–49.

33. Congressman William Wick of Indiana, *Congressional Globe*, 29th Congress, first session (January 30, 1846): 184.

34. See Nicolás Kanellos, "A Socio-Historic Study of Hispanic Newspapers in the United States," in Ramón Gutiérrez and Genrao Padilla, eds. Recove*ring the U.S. Hispanic Literary Heritage* (Houston, Arte Público Press, 1993): 107–128.

35. Matías Montes Hidobro, ed. *El laúd del desterrado,* reprint edition (Houston: Arte Público Press, 1995).

36. Luis Leal and Rodolfo Cortina, *Jicotencal,* reprint edition (Houston: Arte Público Press, 1995).

37. See Gerald Poyo, *"With All, and for the Good of All": The Emergence of Popular Nationalism in the Cuban Communities of the United States, 1848–1898* (Durham, N.C.: Duke University Press, 1989): 1–51.

38. See Jean M. Stubbs, *Tobacco on the Periphery: A Case Study in Cuban Labour History, 1860–1958* (Cambridge, England: Cambridge University Press, 1985): 15–27.

39. Since the Immigration Act of 1917 created the prohibitively high head tax of $7, with other fees added later, both employers and emigrants began facilitating clandestine border crossings. Therefore, there is no estimating how many illegal immigrants came into the United States through the Mexican border during these years.

40. The thesis of overpopulation has been recently challenged by scholars who conclude that workers were encouraged and channeled into emigration by the colonial government. See History Task Force of the Centro de Estudios Puetorriqueños, *Labor Migration under Capitalism: The Puerto Rican Experience* (New York: Monthly Review Press, 1979).

41. See Christopher Mitchell, "Introduction: Immigration and U.S. Foreign Policy toward the Caribbean, Central America and Mexico," *Western Hemisphere Immigration and United States Foreign Policy*, ed. by Christopher Mitchell (University Park, Pa.: Pennsylvania State University Press, 1992).

42. See Clint Wilson, Jr. and Félix F. Gutiérrez, *Minorities and the Media: Diversity and the End of Mass Communication* (Beverly Hills, Calif.: Sage, 1985).

43. See Félix F. Gutiérrez, "Latinos and the Media," *Readings in Mass Communications,* ed. by M Emery and T. C. Smythe (Dubuque, Iowa: W. C. Brown, 1989).

44. See James Evans, "The Indian Savage, the Mexican Bandit and the Chinese Heathen." (Unpublished doctoral dissertation, University of Texas, 1967).

45. See Carey McWilliams, *Blood in the Pavement, North from Mexico* (New York: J. B. Lippincott, 1949); Joshua Fishman and H. Casiano, "Puerto Ricans in Our Press," *Modern Language Journal* 53.3 (1969): 157–162; Ricardo Chavira, "A Case Study: Reporting of Mexican Emigration and Deportation," *Journalism History,* 4.2 (1977): 59–61.

46. See Arthur G. Pettit, *Images of the Mexican American in Fiction and Film* (College Station: Texas A & M University Press, 1980); Allen Woll, *The Latin Image in American Film* (Los Angeles: Latin American Center Publications, University of California, 1980); Charles Ramírez Berg, "Stereotyping in Films in General and of the Hispanic in Particular," *Howard Journal of Communications,* 2.3 (1990): 286–300.

47. *The New York Times,* February 11, 1922.

48. *The New York Times,* September 19, 1926.

49. *The New York Times,* April 3, 1927.

50. *The New York Times,* January 3, 1928.

51. *Variety,* September 3, 1940: 6

52. Gustavo Pérez Firmat has shown how Desi Arnaz encoded into this relationship of an Hispanic buffoon and his Anglo-American love object a much more sophisticated, as well as complicated, metaphor for both Anglo-American racial attitudes and the development of Hispanic-American biculturalism in the United States. See "I-Love-Ricky," in Firmat's *Life on the Hyphen: The Cuban-American Way* (Austin: University of Texas Press, 1994): 23–45.

Bibliography

Acosta-Belén, Edna, ed. *The Puerto Rican Woman.* New York: Praeger, 1986.

Aguilar Camín, Héctor, and Lorenzo Meyer. *In the Shadow of the Mexican Revolution: Contemporary Mexican History, 1910–1989.* Austin: University of Texas Press, 1993.

Alvarez, Robert R. *Famila: Migration and Adaptation in Alta and Baja California, 1850–1975.* Berkeley: University of California Press, 1987.

Ameringer, Charles. *The Democratic Left in Exile: The Antidictatorial Struggle in the Caribbean, 1945–1959.* Coral Gables: University of Miami Press, 1974.

Bannon, John Francis, ed. *The Spanish Borderlands Frontier, 1512–1821.* Norman: University of Oklahoma Press, 1970.

Barrera, Mario. *Race and Class in the Southwest: A Theory of Racial Inequality.* Notre Dame, Ind.: University of Notre Dame Press, 1979.

Bean, Frank D., and Marta Tienda. *The Hispanic Population of the United States.* New York: Russell Sage Foundation, 1988.

Beardsley, John, and Jane Livingston. *Hispanic Art in the United States: Thirty Painters and Sculptors.* New York: Abbeville Press, 1987.

Bennett, Deb, and Robert S. Hoffmann. "Ranching in the New World." In *Seeds of Change: A Quincentennial Commemoration.* Herman J. Viola and Carolyn Margolis, eds. Washington, D.C.: Smithsonian Institution Press, 1991.

Berg, Charles Ramírez. "Stereotyping in Films in General and of the Hispanic in Particular," *Howard Journal of Communications,* 2.3 (1990): 286–300.

Blasier, Cole. *The Hovering Giant: U.S. Responses to Revolutionary Change in Latin America.* Pittsburgh, Pa.: University of Pittsburgh Press, 1979.

Boswell, T. D., and J. R. Curtis. *The Cuban American Experience: Culture, Images and Perspectives.* Totowa, N.J.: Rowman and Allenheld, 1984.

153

Briggs, Vernon M., Jr. *Immigration Policy and the American Labor Force.* Baltimore: The Johns Hopkins University Press, 1984.

Burns, Edward McNall. *The American Idea of Mission.* Westport, Conn.: Greenwood Press, 1973.

Carter, Hodding. *Doomed Road of Empire: The Spanish Trail of Conquest.* New York: McGraw-Hill, 1963.

Castedo, Leopoldo. *A History of Latin American Art and Architecture from Pre-Colombian Times to the Present.* Trans. by Phyllis Freeman. New York: Praeger, 1969.

Cawley, Robert. *Unpathed Waters: Studies in the Influence of the Voyagers on Elizabethan Literature.* Princeton, N.J.: Princeton University Press, 1940.

Chavira, Ricardo. "A Case Study: Reporting of Mexican Emigration and Deportation," *Journalism History,* 4.2 (1977): 59–61.

Chilcote, Ronald S. *Latin America: The Struggle with Dependency and Beyond.* New York: Schenkman, 1974.

Chipman, Donald E. *Spanish Texas, 1519–1821.* Austin: University of Texas Press, 1992.

Collier, Simon. *From Cortés to Castro: An Introduction to the History of Latin America.* New York: Macmillan, 1974.

Divine, Robert A. *American Immigration Policy, 1924–1952.* New Haven, Conn.: Yale University Press, 1957.

Dixon, Marlene. *On Trial: Reagan's War Against Nicaragua.* San Francisco: Synthesis Publications, 1985.

Dobkins, Betty Eakle. *The Spanish Element in Texas Law.* Austin: University of Texas Press, 1959.

Dolan, Jay P., and Allan Figueroa Deck. *Hispanic Catholic Culture in the United States: Issues and Concerns.* Notre Dame, Ind.: University of Notre Dame, 1994.

Dunkerley, James. *Power in the Isthmus: A Political History of Central America.* London: Verso, 1988.

Eaton, John. *The Mind of the Old South.* Baton Rouge: Louisiana State University Press, 1967.

Elson, Ruth Miller. *Guardians of Tradition: Schoolbooks of the Nineteenth Century.* Lincoln: University of Nebraska Press, 1964.

Evans, James. "The Indian Savage, the Mexican Bandit and the Chinese Heathen." Unpublished doctoral dissertation, University of Texas, 1967.

Fagen, Richard R., Richard A. Brody, and Thomas J. O'Leary. *Cubans in Exile: Disaffection and the Revolution.* Stanford, Calif.: Stanford University Press, 1968.

Fishman, Joshua, and H. Casiano. "Puerto Ricans in Our Press," *Modern Language Journal,* 53.3 (1969): 157–162

Fitzpatrick, Joseph P. *The Puerto Rican Americans: The Meaning of Migration to the Mainland.* Englewood Cliffs: Prentice-Hall, 1987.

Fontana, Bernard L. *Entrada: The Legacy of Spain and Mexico in the United States.* Albuquerque: The University of New Mexico Press, 1994.

García, Mario. T. *Mexican Americans.* New Haven, Conn.: Yale University Press, 1989.

García Izcabalceta, Joaquín. *Bibliografía mexicana del siglo XVI.* Mexico: Fondo de Cultura Económica, 1954.

García y Griego, Manuel. "The Importation of Mexican Contract Laborers to the United States." *Between Two Worlds: Mexican Immigrants in the United States.* Ed. by David E. Gutiérrez. Wilmington, Del.: SR Books, 1996, 45–88.

Garner, Jane. "Flying Sheets, Early Newspapers Important to Scholarly Inquiry," *The General Libraries Newsletter,* The University of Texas, 28 (Fall 1987): 3–5.

Gerhard, Peter. *The Northern Frontier.* Princeton, N.J.: Princeton University Press, 1982.

Geyl, Pieter. *The Revolt of the Netherlands (1555–1609),* second edition. London: Benn, 1980.

Gómez-Quiñones, Juan. *Roots of Chicano Politics, 1600–1940.* Albuquerque: University of New Mexico Press, 1994.

Gutiérrez, Félix F. "Latinos and the Media," in *Readings in Mass Communication.* Ed. by M. Emery and T. C. Smythe. Dubuque, Iowa: W. C. Brown, 1989.

———. "Spanish Language Media in America: Background, Resources, History," *Journalism History,* 4/2 (Summer 1977): 34–41.

Henderson, Ann L., and Gary R. Mormino. *Spanish Pathways in Florida.* Sarasota, Fla.: Pineapple Press, 1991.

Hendricks, G. L. *The Dominican Diaspora: From the Dominican Republic to New York City.* New York: Teacher's College Press of Columbia University, 1974.

Henry, O. *Heart of the West.* Garden City, N.Y.: Doubleday, Page & Co., 1919.

Hernández, José M. *Cuba and the United States: Intervention and Militarism, 1868–1933.* Austin: University of Texas Press, 1993.

History Task Force of the Centro de Estudios Puetorriqueños. *Labor Migration under Capitalism: The Puerto Rican Experience.* New York: Monthly Review Press, 1979.

Hoffman, Abraham. *Unwanted Mexican Americans in the Great Depression: Repatriation Pressures.* Tucson: University of Arizona Press, 1974.

✗ Horsman, Reginald. *Race and Manifest Destiny. The Origins of American Racial Anglo-Saxonism.* Cambridge, Mass.: Harvard University Press, 1981.

Juderías, Julián. *La leyenda negra: Estudios acerca del concepto de España en el extranjero,* thirteenth edition. Madrid: Editora Nacional, 1954.

Kanellos, Nicolás. *Hispanic Firsts: 500 Years of Extraordinary Achievement.* Detroit: Gale Research, 1997.

———. *A History of Hispanic Theater in the United States: Origins to 1940.* Austin: University of Texas Press, 1990.

———, ed. *Hispanic American Almanac.* Detroit: Gale Research, 1993.

———, ed. *Biographical Dictionary of Hispanic Literature: The Literature of Puerto Rican Americans, Cuban Americans, and Other Hispanic Writers.* Westport, Conn.: Greenwood Press, 1985.

———. "A Socio-Historic Study of Spanish-Language Newspapers in the United States." In *Recovering the U.S. Literary Heritage.* Ed. by Ramón Gutiérrez and Genaro Padilla. Houston: Arte Público Press, 1993, 107–128.

Kanellos, Nicolás, and Cristelia Pérez. *Chronology of Hispanic American History.* Detroit: Gale Research, 1995.

Kanellos, Nicolás, and Claudio Esteva-Fabregat. General eds. *Handbook of Hispanic Cutlures in the United States.* 4 volumes. Houston: Arte Público Press, 1993–1994.

Keller, Gary. "Film." In *The Hispanic American Almanac.* Ed. by Nicolás Kanellos. Detroit: Gale Research, 1993, 543–594.

Knight, Franklin W. *The Caribbean.* New York: Oxford University Press, 1990.

Korrol, Virginia Sánchez. "In Their Own Right: A History of Puerto Ricans in the U.S." In *Handbook of Hispanic Cultures in the United States: History.* Ed. by Alfredo Jiménez. Houston: Arte Público Press, 1994.

Leonard, Thomas. "Relations with Spain and Spanish America." In *The Hispanic American Almanac.* Ed. by Nicolás Kanellos. Detroit: Gale Research, 1993.

Llanes, J. *Cuban Americans, Masters of Survival.* Cambridge, Mass.: Harvard University Press, 1982.

López, Adalberto, ed. *The Puerto Ricans: Their History, Culture and Society.* Cambridge, Mass.: Schenkman, 1980.

MacLachlan, Colin M. *Spain's Empire in the New World: The Role of Ideas and Social Change.* Berkeley: University of California Press, 1988.

Maltby, William S. *The Black Legend in England: The Development of Anti-Spanish Sentiment, 1558–1660.* Durham, N.C.: Duke University Press, 1971.

Martz, John D., ed. *U.S. Policy toward Latin America: Quarter Century of Crisis and Challenge.* Lincoln: University of Nebraska Press, 1987.

McGroarty, John Steven. *Los Angeles from the Mountains to the Sea.* Chicago and New York: The American Historical Society, 1921.

McKnight, Joseph. "Law without Lawyers on the Hispano Mexican Frontier," *The West Texas Historical Association Yearbook,* 64 (1990): 51–65.

———. *The Spanish Elements in Modern Texas Law.* Dallas: n.p., 1979.

McWilliams, Carey. *Blood in the Pavement, North from Mexico.* New York: J. B. Lippincott, 1949.

Meier, Matt S., Feliciano Rivera. *Dictionary of Mexican American History.* Westport, Conn.: Greenwood Press, 1981.

Meléndez, Edwin, and Edgardo Meléndez, eds. *Colonial Dilemma: Critical Perspectives on Contemporary Puerto Rico.* Boston: South End Press, 1993.

Meyer, Michael C. *Water in the Hispanic Southwest: A Social and Legal History, 1550–1850.* Tucson: University of Arizona Press, 1984.

Mintz, Sidney W. "Pleasure, Profit, and Satiation." In *Seeds of Change: A Quincentennial Commemoration.* Ed. by Herman J. Viola and Carolyn Margolis. Washington, D.C.: Smithsonian Institution Press, 1991.

Mitchell, Christopher. "Introduction: Immigration and U.S. Foreign Policy toward the Caribbean, Central America and Mexico." In *Western Hemisphere Immigration and United States Foreign Policy.* Ed. by Christopher Mitchell. University Park, Pa.: Pennsylvania State University Press, 1992.

Montes Huidobro, Matías, ed. *El laú del desterrado.* Houston: Arte Público Press, 1995.

Moore, Joan, and Harry Pachón. *Hispanics in the United States.* Englewood Cliffs, N.J.: Prentice-Hall, 1985.

Morales, Julio. *Puerto Rican Poverty and Migration: We Just Had to Try Elsewhere.* New York: Praeger, 1986.

Morales Carrión, Arturo, ed. *Puerto Rico: A Political and Cultural History.* New York: W. W. Norton, 1983.

Munro, Dana G. *Intervention and Dolar Diplomacy in the Caribbean.* Princeton, N.J.: Princeton University Press, 1964.

Nicoloff, Philip L. *Emerson on Race and History: An Examination of English Traits.* New York: Columbia University Press, 1961.

Nott, J. C., and George R. Gliddon. *Types of Mankind.* Philadelphia: Lippincott, 1854.

Pedraza-Bailey, S. *Political and Economic Migrants in the America.* Austin: University of Texas Press, 1985.

Pérez, Lisandro. "Immigrant Economic Adjustment and Family Organization: The Cuban Success Story Reexamined," *International Migration Review,* 20 (Spring 1986): 1–20.

Pettit, Arthur G. *Images of the Mexican American in Fiction and Film.* College Station: Texas A & M University Press, 1980.

Portes, Alejandro, and Robert L. Bach. *Latin Journey: Cuban and Mexican Immigrants in the United States.* Berkeley: University of California Press, 1985.

Powell, Philip Wayne. *Tree of Hate: Propaganda and Prejudices Affecting United States Relations with the Hispanic World.* New York: Basic Books, 1971.

Poyo, Gerald. *"With All, and for the good of All": The Emergence of Popular Nationalism in the Cuban Communities of the United States.* Durham, N.C.: Duke University Press, 1989.

Poyo, Gerald E., and Mariano Díaz-Miranda. "Cubans in the United States." In *Handbook of Hispanic Cultures in the United States: History.* Ed. by Alfredo Jiménez. Houston: Arte Público Press, 1994.

Reisler, Mark. "Always the Laborer, Never the Citizen: Anglo Perceptions of the Mexican Immigrant during the 1920's." In *Between Two Worlds: Mexican Immigrants in the United States.* Ed. by David G. Gutiérrez. Wilmington, Del.: SR Books, 1996, 23–43.

Rodríguez-Fraticelli, Carlos, and Amílcar Tirado, "Notes towards a History of Puerto Rican Community Organizations in New York City," *Centro de Estudios Puertorriqueños Bulletin,* 2, 6 (1989): 35–47.

Rosaldo, Renato, Robert A. Calvert, and Gustav L. Seligmann. *Chicano: The Evolution of a People.* Minneapolis: Winston Press, 1973.

Rosales, Arturo. "A Historical Overview." In *The Hispanic American Almanac.* Ed. by Nicolás Kanellos. Detroit: Gale Research, 1993.

Ruiz de Burton, María Amparo. *The Squatter and the Don.* Houston: Arte Público Press, 1993.

Sánchez, Rosaura. *Telling Identities: The Californio Testimonios.* Minneapolis: University of Minnesota Press, 1996.

Senate Committee on Immigration. *Hearings on the Admission of Mexican Agricultural Laborers.* 66th Congress, second session, 1920.

Sheridan, Thomas E. *Los Tucsonenses: The Mexican Community in Tucson.* Tucson: University of Arizona Press, 1986.

Shular, Antonia Castañeda, Tomás Ybarra-Frausto, and Joseph Sommers, eds. *Literatura chicana: Texto y contexto.* Englewood Cliffs, N.J.: Prentice-Hall, 1972.

Simmons, Marc. "Spanish Irrigation Practices in New Mexico," *New Mexico Historical Review,* 47 (April 1972): 138–139.

Simms, William Gilmore. *The Letters of William Gilmore Simms,* 5 volumes. Mary C. Simms Oliphant, Alfred Taylor Odell, and T. C. Duncan Eaves, eds. Columbia: University of South Carolina Press, 1952.

Simons, Helen, and Cathryn A. Hoyt, eds. *Hispanic Texas: A Historical Guide.* Austin: University of Texas Press, 1992.

Slatta, Richard W. *Cowboys of the Americas.* New Haven, Conn.: Yale University Press, 1990.

Stubbs, Jean M. *Tobacco on the Periphery: A Case Study in Cuban Labour History, 1860–1958.* Cambridge, England: Cambridge University Press, 1985.

Subervi-Vélez, Federico A. "Mass Comunication and Hispanics," *Handbook of Hispanic Cultures in the United States: Sociology.* Ed. by Félix Padilla. Houston: Arte Público Press, 1993, 304–357.

Suchlicki, Jaime. *Cuba: From Columbus to Castro.* Washington, D.C.: Pergammon Press, 1986.

Valdez, Dennis. "Labor and Employment." In *The Hispanic American Almanac.* Ed. by Nicolás Kanellos. Detroit: Gale Research, 1993.

Vallejo, Guadalupe. "Ranch and Mission Days in Alta California," *The Century Magazine,* 41, no. 2 (1890): 183.

Viola, Herman J., and Carolyn Margolis, eds. *Seeds of Change: A Quincentennial Commemoration.* Washington, D.C.: Smithsonian Institution Press, 1991.

Weber, David. *The Spanish Frontier in North America.* New Haven, Conn.: Yale University Press, 1992.

———. *Myth and History of the Hispanic Southwest.* Albuquerque: University of New Mexico Press, 1988.

———. *The Mexican Frontier, 1821–1846: The American Southwest under Mexico.* Albuquerque: University of New Mexico Press, 1982.

Wilson, Clint, Jr., and Félix F. Gutiérrez. *Minorities and the Media: Diversity and the End of Mass Communication.* Beverly Hills, Calif.: Sage, 1985.

159

Woll, Allen. *The Latin Image in American Film*. Los Angeles: Latin American Center Publications, University of California, 1980.

Zamora, Emilio. *The World of the Mexican Worker in Texas*. College Station: Texas A & M University Press, 1993.

Index

Index

163

About the Author

Nicolás Kanellos has been professor at the University of Houston since 1980. He is founding publisher of the noted Hispanic literary journal *The Americas Review* (formerly *Revista Chicano-Riqueña*) and the nation's oldest and most esteemed Hispanic publishing house, Arte Público Press. Arté Público Press is the largest nonprofit publisher of literature in the United States.

Recognized for his scholarly achievements, Dr. Kanellos is the recipient of the 1996 Denali Press Award of the American Library Association, the 1989 American Book Award—Publisher/Editor Category, the 1989 award from the Texas Association of Chicanos in Higher Education, the 1988 Hispanic Heritage Award for Literature presented by the White House as well as various fellowships and other recognitions. His monograph, *A History of Hispanic Theater in the United States: Origins to 1940* (1990), received three book awards, including that of the Southwest Council on Latin American Studies.

Dr. Kanellos is the director of a major national research program, Recovering the U.S. Hispanic Literary Heritage of the United States, whose objective is to identify, preserve, study, and make accessible tens of thousands of literary documents of those regions that have become the United States from the colonial period to 1960. In 1994, President Bill Clinton appointed Dr. Kanellos to the National Council on the Humanities. In 1996, he became the first Brown Foundation Professor of Hispanic Literature at the University of Houston.